# THE OFFICIAL

# Leeds United

# FANS' GUIDE

THIS IS A CARLTON BOOK

This edition published in 1997

10 9 8 7 6 5 4 3 2 1



A CIP catalogue record for this book is available from the British Library

ISBN 1 85868 412 9

Project Editor: Martin Corteel
Project art direction: Paul Messam
Production: Garry Lewis and Sarah Schuman
Picture research: Sarah Moule
Designed by Michael Spender

**Author's acknowledgements**
The author wishes to thank the following for their help with this book: Nigel Pleasants, Eddie Gray MBE and Keith Harvey of Leeds United. Sue and the girls in the general and commercial offices at Elland Road. The staff at The British Library and the editorial and research team at Carlton Books. Last, but not least, David Benson for his computer wizardry.

Printed in Italy

THE OFFICIAL

# Leeds United

# FANS' GUIDE

## THE STORY OF THE PREMIER LEAGUE YEARS

COLIN BENSON

CARLTON

# Contents

David Hopkins on the ball in August 1997

George Graham and co. in September 1996

Leeds Utd, winners of the Youth Cup in 1993

Bell
PUMA

# Introduction

**This book essentially traces the club's progress in the FA Premier League, which was introduced in 1992, and thus provides a detailed, up-to-date record of the team's achievements in the 1990s. It is a story of two managers, Howard Wilkinson and George Graham; a story of triumph and disappointment that takes us again to the major stadiums of Europe in the Champions' Cup and to Wembley in the Coca-Cola Cup.**

This was an era greatly influenced by the Bosman ruling, which opened the gates for foreign superstars to come to Britain. Howard Wilkinson wasted no time in bringing the mercurial, often controversial Frenchman Eric Cantona to Elland Road. Eric and a host of other Continental favourites come under the microscope, including the dynamic striker Tony Yeboah, a powerfully-built man with the grace and mobility of a tiger.

The present, of course, is always influenced by the past; and in Leeds United's case it is no secret that the Revie years were the greatest of all. We reflect on these times, and wander through the pages of nostalgia to recall some great games: the victory that earned Leeds their first promotion as second division champions in 1924; their 8–0 hammering of Leicester City in the 1930s; and, in more recent times, the famous victory that ended Liverpool's great unbeaten record at Anfield.

These are great games and great names, such as Gordon Hodgson, who scored five goals against Leicester City; John Charles; Billy Bremner; Johnny Giles; big Jack Charlton; Allan Clarke; Norman "Bite-Your-Legs" Hunter; and the rest of the Revie men. There's also Eddie Gray, who is still on the staff and provides a link between the past and the present. Eddie looks after the youth team and suggests one or two names to look out for in the future.

It might be a trifling fact, but it is true that since Jimmy Hill won the Professional Footballers' Association their first big pay rise 36 years ago, only once has the FA Cup Final not involved a club from London, Manchester or Liverpool. The exception was in 1973, when Leeds and Sunderland performed the honours. United are a big club and the fans think it is high time they returned. Howard Wilkinson did get to Wembley in the League Cup and went a long way towards banishing the ghost of Revie by winning the League Championship. But he couldn't maintain the image; and now it is down to George Graham to try and recapture the glory years.

The new boss has something of a reputation, but then so too did some of his predecessors. George, who is fascinated by history, will not have lost sight of the fact that, as at Highbury, he is once again following in the footsteps of the great Herbert Chapman.

There have been other men of stature too, such as Major Frank Buckley, a fitness fanatic who installed a mechanical kicking machine which spat balls out at varying heights and speeds. He was the celebrated "monkey-gland" man; and, according to one former player, Eric Kerfoot, not a person everyone took to immediately.

That was the glorious past. But with exciting new developments planned for Elland Road and George Graham beginning to make his mark, Leeds United also look set for a rewarding future.

**Wise buy: United paid £2.25 million for 'keeper Nigel Martyn – and he proved to be worth every penny**

# Chapter 1
# The History of United

**Although the city is now home to one of England's most famous clubs, Association football had a difficult start in Leeds. And Leeds United had been in the Football League for some 40 years before they began to make their presence felt among the best in the country, under the guidance of manager Don Revie.**

**Little Arthur Hydes, former toffee factory worker, created many sticky moments for the opposition**

The name of Don Revie will forever be linked with Leeds' halcyon days, for under his stewardship, between 1961–74, the club enjoyed its most rewarding period, becoming not only a household name but the flagship of English soccer.

Up until then, the Peacocks had hardly ruffled any feathers, the second division championship win in 1924 being their biggest prize. But Leeds United's eventual success emerged from a veritable vortex which threatened to destroy the game in the city. In this respect it is interesting to relate the tribulations of Association Football in Leeds, whose birth and development in a rugby stronghold afford one of the most amazing stories in the history of the game.

One should not, of course, associate the Leeds United club with the one which preceded it as the occupant of Elland Road; for the old Leeds City club, the outcast and alleged black sheep of the wartime flock, was as dead as a door-nail.

So the city of Leeds looked like being bereft of a first-class Association football club after the First World War. Association football had been pioneered in the area by Hunslet, whose players and supporters formed Leeds City in 1904 and fielded an experimental team before gaining acceptance to the second division of the Football League in 1905.

**The Leeds United team from the 1914–15 season. John Hampson (second from right – back row) and Billy McLeod (centre – front row) were auctioned by the Football League**

They had to seek re-election on one occasion, but apart from that, everything seemed to be going well. After the break for the 1914–18 war City started the season encouragingly. They had several old favourites on view in "Mick" Foley, ace scorer Billy McLeod and Simpson Bainbridge, but then came rumours of trouble with the authorities and charges of making illegal payments during the war years.

It came as a sudden shock, for there was a widespread feeling in Yorkshire that should Leeds City be expelled from the League, as was threatened, it would be a severe setback for the game in the West Riding.

## *City suspended*

At first, the club stood suspended, and could not fulfil its fixture with South Shields on Saturday 11 October 1919. Despite the seriousness of the situation there was a glimmer of hope. The Lord Mayor of Leeds, Joseph Henry, a strong supporter of the club, made laudable efforts to keep City alive and was instrumental in reopening the inquiry into allegations of excessive payment of players during wartime and offers being made to registered players of other clubs. Alas, his advances to the Football Association did not meet with the desired result.

The case against Leeds City was still unproven, but while certain documents relating to the affairs of the club remained concealed the authorities had little alternative but to suspend the club.

The fate of City lay in the hands of those who were parties to the concealing of the documents, and as they observed a mutual agreement of silence the outcome, which was the worst that could befall the club, was inevitable. Leeds City were expelled from the Football League.

The football folk of Leeds were stunned and their disappointment and frustrations were increased a week later when a scene unique in the annals of professional football was enacted at the Hotel Metropole. For here, the Football League held an auction of City players.

More than 30 League clubs were represented and presented with a list of minimum fees required by the League sub-committee staging the event. It read as follows: Billy McLeod, Harry Millership, John Hampson and Simpson Bainbridge £1,000 each; Willis Walker, Tom Lamph and John Edmondson £800 each; Arthur Price £750; and so on down to Matthews and Chiperfield, who had not played in the first team, who were available at £100 each.

There was a complaint that some fees were far too high and so the organisers agreed to accept the highest bids, made in sealed envelopes by the clubs. The committee stressed to the players that they did not have to go to the highest bidder if they did not wish, that the decision would be theirs entirely, but that everything was being done in their interests. In the end, McLeod went to Notts County, Walker and Hopkins to South Shields and Hampson and Kirton to Aston Villa, while Bainbridge signed for Preston.

## *Hello United*

The stark reality that Leeds City was dead prompted football enthusiasts to act. Within hours of the auction some 1,000 fans gathered at the Salem Hall where local solicitor Alf Masser chaired a meeting which proposed the formation of a professional club. A seven-man committee was elected, comprising Masser, Joe Henry Junior (son of the mayor), Mark Barker, Charles Snape, R.E.H. Ramsden and former players Charles Morgan and Dick Ray, who was to be installed as the club's first manager.

**Hilton Crowther who transferred his allegiance and his cash from Huddersfield Town to Leeds United**

Their enthusiasm was boosted by an invitation to Leeds United to take over the city's reserve-team fixtures in the Midland League, and by the actions of the Yorkshire Amateurs, now residing at Elland Road, who graciously offered to make way for the newly-constituted United.

Then a thunderbolt was dropped on the West Riding. Huddersfield Town's wealthy chairman, Hilton Crowther, proposed to transfer his club "lock, stock and barrel" from Leeds Road to Elland Road. Disillusioned with the support his club was getting, he saw Leeds, which then boasted a population of 400,000, as an ideal catchment area.

No greater crisis, surely, than the one contained in this proposal, ever confronted the Association game in two great footballing centres. It required all the native pride of the people of Huddersfield to defeat that project, the only sequel to which was the transfer of Hilton Crowther's financial interests from Huddersfield to Leeds. There was so much fierce and bitter controversy; yet, with hindsight, could it not be claimed as a blessing in disguise?

Certainly, Huddersfield Town never looked back and enjoyed greater success than in the 1920s following its reconstruction under Stonor Crowther (same family), who retained a controlling interest; and Leeds United climbed into the same company, their second-division championship success in 1924 giving the West Riding two first-division clubs where there might have been only one.

This was not only a grand thing for Leeds but for the development of the game in Yorkshire, whatever rift there might have been among the supporters at Elland Road.

Some of them wanted to discharge the debt owing to Hilton Crowther, who in the creation of Leeds United and the realization of an ambition had reportedly invested between £35,000 and £40,000, (which of course gave him a control to which he was fully entitled, on the principle that he who pays the piper calls the tune). It was understood, however, that he was willing to relinquish that control in the event of promotion being won; and conditional, naturally, on his holding in the club being bought back.

Whatever the criticism, Hilton Crowther played an enormous part in bringing first-division football to Leeds, the last of the major English cities to secure it. His first crucial appointment had been that of Arthur

**The Leeds United team from 1923–24, the season that they earned promotion to the first division**

Fairclough as secretary/manager, an experienced leader with a great reputation as a star-maker and, above all, with a record of twice getting his previous club, Barnsley, elected to the League.

Fairclough announced: "The plan to be pursued is to secure a blend of youth and experience." Among the youngsters he introduced were outside-left Jerry Best of Newcastle United, a cousin of Huddersfield favourite "Bobby" Best, and James Walton, a wing-half-back from West Stanley. For Billy Down, the goalkeeper from Ashington, Sunderland were previously asked £1,000; and experience was provided by the likes of Huddersfield half-back James Baker and centre-half Ernie Hart.

On 31 May 1920 Leeds United were elected to the second division of the Football League, polling 31 votes. Cardiff joined them in the League with 23 votes while Grimsby, Lincoln and Walsall failed in their applications.

United made their Football League debut at Port Vale on Saturday 28 August 1920; an ironic twist, for Vale had taken over City's League fixtures on their expulsion. But there was to be no fairy-tale start for Leeds, who lost 2–0 with the following line-up: Down; Duffield, Tillotson; Musgrove, Baker, Walton; Mason, Goldthorpe, Thompson, Lyon, Best.

Len Armitage replaced Robert Thompson at centre-forward for the second game and goes down in the record-books as the scorer of United's first League goal. It wasn't enough, however, South Shields winning 2–1. The return game with Port Vale was next and Leeds recorded their first win, 3–1.

United finished 14th in that first season, Thompson top scorer with 11 goals. They quickly improved, occupying the eighth and then the seventh rung on the ladder before topping the table in 1924. Percy Whipp (11 goals), Joe Richmond (15 goals) and Jack Swann (18 goals) had been forged into a formidable front trio and Leeds was no longer in the backwash of football; it was now in the swim with the most famous clubs in the land and an immense new adventure lay before it, despite the fact that the main sporting interest in the area remained rugby. But with a great population to draw on, first-division football now had a chance to make an impact. The strongest side during that Championship campaign was: Down; Duffield, Menzies; Sherwin, Hart, Baker; Coats, Whipp, Richmond, Swann, Harris.

**The Leeds team battles it out with London club Queens Park Rangers in January 1932**

Leeds opened their first-division account with a 1–1 home draw against Sunderland on 30 August 1924, Swann netting the first of his 11 League goals in a season of strife. Only a late flourish of three wins in the last five games kept them safe. It was even tighter the following year, a 4–1 home win over Spurs in the final match providing salvation. But they couldn't avoid the drop a third time, even though Tom Jennings rattled in 35 goals, so Leeds suffered the humiliation of relegation for the first time in April 1927. Dick Ray then took over the managerial reins from Arthur Fairclough and United returned to the top flight at the first attempt as runners-up to Manchester City, with a club record 98 goals; Jennings (21), White (21), Wainscoat (18) and young Charlie Keetley, who scored 18 goals in 16 League appearances, were the top shots.

In the 1929–30 season, Leeds finished fifth in Division One – the club's best League standing before the Revie days. A major tightening-up of the defence had provided a sound foundation and there was a genuine hope in the Leeds camp that United were on the brink of true greatness. Yet, inexplicably, they slid back into Division Two.

Runners-up again in 1932, Leeds stayed in Division One until the Second World War without making any significant impact, and upon resumption of the League programme in the 1946–47 campaign relied on many of the men who had served them in the late 1930s. They were well past their play-by date and this was reflected clearly in the performances. United collected only 18 points, the second lowest of all time, losing 15 and drawing the other two of their last 17 fixtures to finish bottom. They called on three goalkeepers, Hodgson, Fernley and Twomey, and three centre-forwards, Henry, Ainsley and Clarke, in desperate attempts to reverse the situation, but it was all to no avail.

New manager Willis Edwards couldn't turn the tide as an uncomfortable season was experienced in Division Two. United escaped the plunge to Division Three (N) by a mere two points, a 5–1 beating of Bury on the final day proving just enough, thanks to a hat-trick from Albert Wakefield and two goals from David Cochrane. To add to the team's poor statistics came a depressing balance sheet which showed United clearly in the red. Major Frank Buckley, freshly installed as manager, opted for youth, and one of his finds was a young man we will hear more about later, John Charles.

The Welsh teenager couldn't make much impression early on, however, and a new low was hit when

**John CHARLES**

**"Big John" was an awesome figure; perfect physique, the balance, control and perception of a Don Revie, with pace to boot. Leeds signed him for £10 as an amateur and he made his League debut, at centre-half, in April 1949. Twelve months later he was the youngest player ever to represent Wales. When Major Frank Buckley switched him to centre-forward for the 1952–53 season he scored 26 goals and set a Club record for the next season, topping the League list with 42. Juventus paid a British record £65,000 to make him "Il Buon Gigante", in April 1957 and he became the most idolized player in Europe. He rejoined Leeds in 1962.**

Leeds toppled out of the FA Cup following an embarrassing 3–1 home defeat by Newport County. But youth needs experience and time, and gradually Buckley began to mould a team together which suggested it was capable of greater achievement. But they flattered to deceive and never produced the consistency required of a promotion outfit. Even when John Charles smashed the club scoring record with 42 goals in 1953–54, United finished only 10th in Division Two.

# Get Carter

Raich Carter came on the scene to achieve what Buckley couldn't, leading United to promotion in 1955–56. Charles was developing into a super athlete. Jack Charlton, though ragged at the edges, was proving a competent defender, while Harold Brook and Albert Nightingale held it all together from inside forward. Here was a team that knew it was going places. Elland Road became a fortress as they stretched their unbeaten home record to 34 games, until Blackburn Rovers burst the bubble in March. United responded with six straight wins, scoring 20 goals and conceding only four, to overhaul Liverpool and claim the runners'-up spot behind Sheffield Wednesday.

In later years, John Charles remembered this promotion campaign as the most exciting he ever experienced. In that lilting Welsh accent he recalled: "It was the most exciting, and exacting, season I ever had in football. We were not among the fancied sides and seemed to be drifting as usual until we ran into the sort of consistent form which is worth far more than all your periodic sensational performances put together. Before anyone realized what was happening we had sneaked our way through the field, and when we finished our last match with a win at Hull, we were back in the first division."

Incidentally, this was the fourth time Leeds had won promotion in a leap year. It proved a leap well within their capabilities for, on their return to Division One, they finished a comfortable eighth. Charles again was outstanding, strong and powerful, a committed competitor who physically intimidated defenders into submission. He netted 38 goals in 40 League games, including two hat-tricks against Sheffield Wednesday, home and away.

Charles became the target of Juventus, and the Italian giants eventually persuaded Leeds to part company with him for a then world record £65,000 in May 1957. The money was well invested in a new stand, but there was nobody to fill the Welshman's boots. Results began to mirror this and a period of instability rocked Elland Road. Carter was sacked; chief coach Bill Lambton took his place only to find himself out in the cold a few months later, ousted by the arrival of Jack Taylor who could not avert the impending slide. In 1960, United again suffered the ignominy of relegation.

**John Charles. He was a powerhouse athlete with exceptional skills and a soft, gentle personality. He won the Italian League twice with Juventus**

**Don Revie believed strongly in the family unit and loyalty, and was like a protective father to his players**

# *Revie arrives*

Despite a summer clearout, United looked a very ordinary second-division outfit when the directors appointed Don Revie as player-manager in March 1961. Little did they realize they had hired the man who would put Leeds United on the European football map.

The club had a £100,000 overdraft at the time, so there was no cash for Revie to invest. In his first full season he flirted with relegation, and only a 3–0 victory at Newcastle on the final day of the 1961–62 campaign secured their tenure in Division Two. Revie himself played only seven times.

In March of that year, Revie paid Everton £25,000 for a 31-year-old Scottish international midfielder. Bobby Collins was to be the catalyst of the Revie revival and captained Leeds to the second-division title in 1964. Around him Revie provided youthful exuberance with the likes of Norman Hunter, Paul Reaney and Billy Bremner. Teenager Gary Sprake replaced Younger in goal and kept 17 clean sheets; Willie Bell and Jack Charlton provided the experience at the back; and the final piece of the jigsaw was the capture of Johnny Giles from Manchester United, a real bargain at £32,000. Giles was an orthodox winger but later formed a world-class midfield partnership with Bremner.

Revie, a great tactician, played 34-year-old Bobby Collins alongside 20-year-old Billy Bremner in the middle of a 4–2–4 formation which was then in its infancy in this country. They gelled like a dream and, with the fleet-footed South African Albert Johanneson operating on the opposite flank to Giles, they created plenty of opportunities for strikers Don Weston and Ian Lawson, a former Burnley prodigy. Leeds started the promotion race from behind, as the opening day fixture at Northampton was postponed because of a cricket match on the County Ground. But wins over Rotherham and Bury provided a comfortable start and a 3–0 win at Northampton on 1 October sparked a run of eight successive away wins. It was second-placed Sunderland who ended a sequence of 20 unbeaten matches on 28 December.

The team were unbeaten all season at home and lost only three second-division games, the other two defeats coming at Preston (who were third) and Manchester City (sixth). An injury to Charlton was overcome when Freddie Goodwin and then teenager Paul Madeley filled the breach, and Revie strengthened his attack in February by signing England striker Alan Peacock from Middlesbrough.

**Billy Bremner, recruited from Scottish junior football, demonstrates his mastery of the ball**

**Jack CHARLTON**

**Don Revie fashioned "Big Jack" into a World Cup winner. A lazy trainer, his career was going nowhere until the Don coaxed the best out of him. He signed as an amateur from Ashington Welfare in 1950. After National Service with the Household Cavalry, he succeeded John Charles at centre-half (1955–56), having made the first of his 629 League appearances (70 goals), against Doncaster on 25 April 1953. A great personality, he became notorious for positioning himself directly in front of goalkeepers at corner kicks. He would have been captain but for a superstition about being last on to the pitch.**

**Johnny Giles, the artistic Dubliner whose passes painted a thousand thrills. He was given away by Manchester United and Revie converted him from the wing to midfield where, alongside Bremner, he orchestrated the side**

**Billy BREMNER**

**Winning was everything to this pint-sized wing-half whose partnership with Johnny Giles was at the heart of Revie's great, great sides. If ever a player wore his heart on his sleeve it was Billy, who was rejected by Arsenal and Chelsea for being "too small". The fiery side of his nature often eclipsed his true talent. Tough-tackling ball-winner as he was, he read the game superbly, was a fine passer and a cool finisher, as his 90 goals in 586 (1) League appearances suggest. He won 54 Scottish caps and captained club and country. He was Footballer of the Year in 1970 and won the UEFA/Fairs Cup in 1967–68 and 1970–71.**

## *Back at the top*

Promotion was clinched with a win at Swansea and the championship signed, sealed and delivered with a 2–0 triumph at Charlton on the last day of the season. The title was won on the back of a mean defence, but could they reproduce the same sort of consistency in the first division?

Yes. Revie's men took the big boys by storm and were well-placed to achieve the hitherto-impossible dream of a League and Cup double until the final countdown. The 1964–65 season opened with three straight wins as Aston Villa, Liverpool and Wolves all succumbed to Revie's hard-working combination. A 2–1 home victory over Sunderland on 26 January 1965 gave Leeds pole position for the first time ever in Division One and they had extended their unbeaten League and Cup run to 25 games when Manchester United, their nearest rivals, put the brakes on with a 1–0 victory at Elland Road on 17 April. It was a defeat that swung the title towards Old Trafford, though a 3–0 defeat at Hillsborough and a 3–3 draw at Birmingham eventually cost Leeds their chance of ultimate glory.

Revie was rewarded with a seven-year contract as he took Leeds into Europe (this is covered in a separate chapter) but his attention to detail and the emphasis he placed on the development of young players was to take United to even greater heights.

The team continued to do well in the League and Cup competitions, though there were some grumbles from other quarters about the tough, physical commitment of the players. Revie had organized his defence well. They were uncompromising and resolute, everyone a defender when the ball was lost, everyone an attacker when in possession. The emphasis was on competitiveness, and only in later years would the players develop more wholly and begin to express their undoubted talents more fluently.

The emergence of talents such as Peter Lorimer, Eddie Gray and Paul Madeley confirmed the brilliant work being done at youth level. They all played a part in helping the 1966–67 side, ravaged by injuries, finish fourth and so qualify for Europe again.

## *Simply the best*

The following season brought the first major trophy to Elland Road, the League Cup. The victory over Arsenal at Wembley was a dull, uninspiring game remembered only for Terry Cooper's winning goal. But it was the breakthrough. Leeds were no longer second-best: they were winners at last.

Mick Jones, United's first ever £100,000 recruit, was bought from Sheffield United to add punch to the attack. A strong, determined runner, he had more skill than he was given credit for, and would eventually form an exciting partnership with Allan Clarke who signed from Leicester City in the summer of 1969. Prior to this, Jones hit 14 goals in the 1968–69 season as Leeds at last won the League title which had eluded them so irritatingly year after year. Second, second, fourth and fourth had been the finishing positions up until now.

Champions! And worthy of the title, too. Only two defeats, at Manchester City and Burnley; a 28-match unbeaten run and a record 67 points in the bag. A goalless draw at Anfield in the penultimate game assured Revie of the title and a Johnny Giles goal against Nottingham Forest two days later completed that record points haul.

Gary Sprake and his defence kept 24 clean sheets and other ever-present selections were Reaney at right-back, Bremner and Hunter. The regular team was: Sprake; Reaney, Cooper, Bremner, Charlton (missed one game), Hunter, O'Grady, Madeley, Jones, Giles, Gray.

**Peter Lorimer scores United's first in a 2–2 draw at Stamford Bridge, beating England's Peter Bonetti**

# *Treble-seekers*

It's tough at the top, and Revie felt no team could afford to lose more than four games if they were to be champions; but such was the success of his phenomenal eleven that 1969–70 saw Leeds chasing glory on three fronts.

Burnley's 48-year-old record was smashed when Leeds stretched their unbeaten League run to 34 games. Everton ended the sequence with a 3–2 win at Goodison Park on 30 August, but it was four months before Leeds suffered another defeat, at Newcastle (2–1). However, as the season reached its climax, United suffered dearly for their own success. At Easter they were poised to win the League, the FA Cup and the European Cup. It proved too many games, too much travelling and too much pressure.

Southampton hammered a nail in United's League aspirations by grabbing a surprise win at Elland Road, and Revie virtually conceded the title to Everton by fielding a complete reserve side at Derby on Easter Monday. United lost 4–1 and were fined £5,000 by the FA for not fielding their strongest available team. You could sense a dullness about the play now, the players suffering more from mental exhaustion than physical exertion. Celtic took full advantage in the European Cup while Chelsea got the rub of the green in the Cup with a disputed David Webb header winning the first FA Cup Final replay since 1912. Eventually Leeds had to be content with the "gallant runners-up" tag once again.

There were more disappointments to follow. Arsenal squeezed Leeds out of the title in 1971 to win the double, the 64 points gathered by the Peacocks the most ever accumulated by a side finishing second under the "two points for a win" rule. It could have all been so different.

Leeds led the first division until a controversial 2–1 home defeat by West Brom on 17 April. This tension-filled afternoon hinged on an outrageous decision by referee Ray Tinkler when he allowed an Albion player who was clearly offside to go on and create a goal. I met Ray the following Monday at Peterborough United, when he admitted he had got it wrong. It had been a bad day for him all round, for he took his wife shopping in Leeds on the Saturday morning and she had spent a fortune on a new coat. Let's say he wasn't in the best frame of mind that afternoon.

United wrapped up the programme with three wins and no goals conceded, including a 1–0 defeat of Arsenal thanks to a Jack Charlton goal. But that Albion fiasco had sunk them. The Gunners nicked the title with a last-gasp goal at Spurs.

**Mick Jones, a strong competitive centre-forward, seen here launching an attack on the Manchester United goal in 1969, was the perfect foil for Allan Clarke's more delicate gifts**

# *Free spirits*

For years, Revie's teams had been labelled functional rather than flamboyant, dour rather than entertaining, by those who did not support the team. It was an image Revie dearly wanted to dispel, for he knew better than anyone the true worth of the players in his charge.

There seemed a new-found freedom in the 1971–72 campaign. Whether this was a conscious effort on the part of the gaffer to get his players to express themselves more, or just a natural maturity on the part of the players, one cannot say. But Leeds were now inspiring viewers not through their professionalism, their thorough organization and crunching tackles, but through the fluency of their play, their skills and mastery of the ball and opponents.

Forced to play the first four home games at neutral grounds following crowd trouble the previous season, they returned to Elland Road determined to put on a show. And how! In the 17 games played on home soil, Leeds dropped just two points and overwhelmed many opponents.

A Jones hat-trick paved the way for the 5–1 defeat of Manchester United; it was Lorimer's turn for three in the total eclipse of Southampton when Bremner, Giles, Lorimer, Clarke, Jones, Madeley and company took the rise out of the Saints with passing movements of up to 20-odd touches in the 7–0 demolition. And Nottingham Forest suffered a 6–1 mauling. These super exhibitions of football at its majestic best were enjoyed and appreciated by a vast television audience.

Leeds won the FA Cup that May, "Sniffer" Clarke's 15th goal of the season proving too much for Arsenal, but missed out on the League again when, 48 hours later, they failed to get the win at Wolves that would have sewn up a famous double.

United, unbalanced by long-term injuries to Terry Cooper and Eddie Gray, finished 1972–73 third. It was their lowest League position for five years.

# *Revie's fitting farewell*

Twelve months later Yorkshire was crowning its heroes as champions again, a fitting climax to Revie's reign. This was vintage Leeds; all-conquering, all-powerful. Maximum points were taken from the first seven games and by Boxing Day, United were nine points clear of the pack. It was Stoke City who inflicted the first defeat of the season in late February, when there was a wobble in form, but Revie rallied the troops and the title was won before the final-day celebrations at Queens Park Rangers which hailed Allan Clarke's 13th goal of the season.

The regular team that year was: Harvey; Reaney, Cherry; Bremner, Madeley, McQueen, Hunter; Lorimer, Clarke, Jones/Jordan, Giles/Yorath.

With Revie off to manage the England side Brian Clough, one of the biggest names in the game, was offered the chance to take Leeds a step further. To the layman, it seemed a perfect choice, but proved a disaster. The players, brought up under the fatherly protection of Revie and used to thorough and meticulous planning for matches, could not come to terms with the off-the-cuff, get-on-and-play style of the new boss, whom they seldom saw. The marriage was a short one, lasting just 44 days.

"Gentleman" Jimmy Armfield held office for the next four years but did not enjoy the best of fortune. Unlucky in the European Cup Final at the end of his first season, he had inherited a team with ageing players, but with the help of Don Howe he refashioned the side and introduced some colourful characters, such as Duncan McKenzie, Tony Currie and Brian Flynn. They played some attractive football, but the best League position United could manage was fifth, not good enough to keep him in his job.

Jock Stein's brief spell was followed by Jimmy Adamson, sacked in September 1980 after a dismal run. Leeds now turned to the old boys to try and rekindle the glories of the 1970s, with Allan Clarke followed by Eddie Gray, then Billy Bremner; but none could match Revie's achievements. Clarke paid a record £930,000 to West Brom for England winger Peter Barnes; Gray brought back Peter Lorimer as captain and gave youth its chance, while Bremner built from the back with a five-man defence and came closest to glory, just missing out on the FA Cup Final in 1987 – beaten 3-2 after extra time by Coventry City in the semi-final – and on the play-off for promotion to Division One thanks to Charlton Athletic, 2-1 winners in a replay.

**Lee CHAPMAN**

**He had an instinctive eye for the target. It was "Chappy's" goal at Bournemouth – his 12th in 21 League appearances – that clinched the second-division championship in 1990. Signed from Nottingham Forest for £400,000 in January 1990 he made the most of his 6ft 3ins in the air. He converted another 21 goals in the first season back in the top flight and netted 16 in the League Championship success in 1991–92. Lee maintained his consistency in the first Premiership campaign with 13 more goals, but at the age of 33 he made way for Brian Deane when sold to Portsmouth for £250,000 in August 1993. Lee registered 80 goals in all competitions for Leeds.**

# *Wilko the saviour*

Impatient for success and following another poor start (United were 21st), Leeds axed Bremner in October 1988 and he was replaced by Howard Wilkinson, the Sheffield Wednesday boss. One of the top coaches in the country, Wilkinson guided the team to sixth place, but they could not sustain the challenge, and ended the season on the seventh rung of the second-division ladder.

Realizing he needed quality players, Wilkinson swooped just before the transfer deadline to make one of the greatest signings of his life: Gordon Strachan, a snip at £300,000 from Manchester United. Also brought in was centre-half Chris Fairclough, who cost £500,000 from Tottenham.

Wilkinson extended his team-building during the summer. John Hendrie arrived from Newcastle for £600,000; Mel Sterland from Rangers for £650,000; and the one that surprised everyone, Vinnie Jones, the self-confessed Wimbledon hard-nut, who cost another £600,000.

Wilkinson used his players effectively, and by December 1989 Leeds were leading the second division. New names hit the headlines: Lee Chapman and Bobby Davison, netting 23 goals between them; Gary Speed, who got his chance when Chris Kamara and David Batty were both suspended; and Peter

Haddock, who also contributed positively.

Chapman's 12th goal, in his 21st League appearance, secured a 1–0 win at Bournemouth on the last day of the season that sealed the championship on goal difference from Sheffield United, with a club record 85 points.

Leeds were back in the big time and Wilkinson intended keeping them there. He splashed out £1 million on goalkeeper John Lukic, Chris Whyte was recruited from WBA, but most crucial of all was the arrival of Scottish captain Gary McAllister. A playmaker supreme, he was to play a major role in Wilkinson's finest hour.

# *Champions again*

After finishing fourth in the 1990–91 season, Leeds swallowed up the League Championship in '92. A classic 4–1 win at Villa took United top in November and in the final furlong it was a two-horse race with the old enemy, Manchester United. Leeds had points in the bag, the Reds games in hand. The signing of Eric Cantona proved a masterly stroke and in the end Leeds won their first Championship in 18 years.

Lukic kept 20 clean sheets, while Chapman scored 16 goals and Rod Wallace 11. The regulars were: Lukic; Sterland/Newsome, Dorigo, Batty, Fairclough, Whyte, Strachan, Wallace, Chapman, McAllister, Speed.

Alas, the following season it all went sour. United flopped in the European Cup, failed to win an away game in the inaugural Premiership and only just avoided the humiliation of relegation.

**"Gentleman" Jimmy Armfield, a former England captain, was able to bring a soothing influence to the club after Brian Clough's turbulent 44 days at Elland Road**

# The Premiership Years

## *Chapter 2*

**Leeds United entered the FA Premiership as Football League champions with a 2–1 home win over Wimbledon on 15 August 1992. In five years of competition they have twice finished fifth and maintained a reputation as one of the more fashionable contenders**

## 1992–93

Leeds United proudly bounced into the newly-formed FA Premier League as Football League champions on 15 August 1992; the euphoria of the previous May's celebrations, when some 300,000 turned out to salute their heroes on their open-topped bus tour of the city, was now a distant memory.

Howard Wikinson's message to the sea of humanity thronging that three-mile cavalcade was: "We'll bring you more of the same."

Wilkinson had lifted United from the foot of Division Two to the very pinnacle of English soccer in just 42 months, a tribute to his organization, tactical prowess and shrewdness in an unstable transfer market. The squad, orchestrated by that golden trio Gordon Strachan, David Batty and Gary McAllister, was playing sweet music. There were tangible grounds for optimism, genuine hopes of a new era of unbridled success.

This was a team of style, speed and stamina; and having brought back the championship for the first time in 18 years, they deserved the recognition afforded them. Unlike the often-reviled Revie machine of the 1960s and '70s, the achievements of Wilkinson's team could not be distorted by charges of over-robust play, for he had rediscovered an era of imaginative artists.

Eric Cantona, a 25-year-old French international, had entered like a gladiator and was already a cult hero after just three months, while the diminutive figure of Rod Wallace had profited from the physical presence of top scorer Lee Chapman, providing the perfect foil. Perhaps the celebrations meant more to local boys Batty and Gary Speed, who like the England midfielder was a graduate of the United youth ranks. Batty, then 22, remarked: "I'm just a supporter who has been lucky enough to realize my ambition to play for the team I love."

It was all grand stuff; though experienced goalkeeper John Lukic, well aware of the fact that once you win a championship you are immediately defending the next, openly lodged a plea to strengthen the team. He explained: "It's not a case of seeing ourselves put out to grass, it's just a fact of life in top-level football, and what the manager must do to keep us at the top is buy and buy big.

"In the dressing-room we are totally realistic about what has to be done in the future. We know we will need a strong squad to build on this success and we accept the gaffer might want to buy three or four new

**Determined Lee Chapman got two goals against Wimbledon on the opening day of the 1992–93 season**

players."

True, Wilkinson had faced bigger selection headaches than any of his main rivals during the championship campaign; and with participation in the European Cup heaping further demands on resources, a squad of real depth was essential if progress (and the defence of the champions' crown) was to be achieved. The boss knew the score, but deflected speculation with a joke. "Maradona would be one. Also Van Basten … But I am not sure about Gullit yet", he chuckled.

## Charity Shield victory

There was a familiar look to the United squad which opened the new season. For the Charity Shield at Wembley against Liverpool, and the opening Premier League fixture, at home to Wimbledon, the same names were on duty as had been on view on the final day of the previous campaign. Lukic in goal; a back line of Newsome, Fairclough, Whyte and Dorigo; Batty, McAllister, Speed, Cantona; and Chapman and Wallace spearheading the attack. The substitutes were still Strachan and Hodge.

Cantona claimed the headlines with a flamboyant hat-trick in a 4–3 victory over Liverpool, a super strike from Tony Dorigo providing the other goal; while Lee Chapman took up where he left off with a brace of goals in the 2–1 victory over Wimbledon.

A 4–1 loss at Middlesbrough cast dark shadows over United's potential, but then in the very next game Eric Cantona magicked up another three goals during a 5–0 demolition of Tottenham Hotspur and it seemed everything was back on track. It wasn't, of course, and successive 2–2 draws with Liverpool and then Oldham Athletic, followed by a 2–0 defeat at Old Trafford, did sow seeds of doubt.

It was Steve Hodge, one of English football's forgotten men, who rose from the bench to score an equalizer in the 1–1 home draw with Aston Villa, but Leeds had lost more than just two points. Injuries to

Chris Whyte heads home to make it 3–1 against Sheffield United

Dorigo and Rod Wallace looked likely to rule them out of the Euro trip to Stuttgart; and when the squad returned from Germany Wilkinson found himself without Newsome, Cantona and Wallace for the tough trip to Southampton.

Gary Speed's late strike at the Dell salvaged a point, but just two wins in nine Premier League outings – 11 points from a possible 27 – was hardly the stuff of champions. Already Leeds found themselves on the slippery slope to becoming also-rans. It was a familiar pattern. Since Wolverhampton Wanderers took the championship honours in 1958 and 1959, only one club – Liverpool – had managed to retain the title, and they had succeeded on three occasions (Manchester United, of course, have subsequently joined this élite band).

## Feeling the strain

Gary McAllister was already feeling the strain. He gasped: "In the last couple of weeks, I've played in an international, two live TV games, travelled into Europe and now come to Southampton." United rediscovered their goal touch with a comprehensive 4–1 victory over Scunthorpe United in the Coca-Cola Cup, and then McAllister's successful penalty conversion against Everton sparked the best performance of the season thus far, "Chappy" Chapman netting his sixth goal in a 2–0 victory.

The grit and determination that had been the key to the championship was now visible again. Wilko said: "I've been barking, growling, pushing, cursing, cajoling and even sweet-talking them over the opening weeks." Yet apart from Scott Sellars, who stood in for the injured Jon Newsome, the manager, despite investing a club record £2 million in former Arsenal winger David Rocastle, refrained from injecting new blood into the side.

Indeed, the Rocastle saga was one of the mysteries of the season; for despite sitting on the bench almost every week, he was not called upon to make a substitute appearance until 3 October at Ipswich, and in total was to make just 11 starts and seven sub appearances all season. Miracle man Gordon Strachan was back in his old routine after a revolutionary back operation, yet influential as he was on the side – and sensationally inspirational in United's glorious triumph over European Cup rule-breakers Stuttgart in Barcelona – one felt the team needed an injection of fresh talent to reawaken its soul.

When Leeds were swept out of Europe by Glasgow Rangers in a tie billed as the "Battle of Britain", rumblings of discontent began to emerge. Rumours of a clash between the gaffer and Cantona were rife and culminated in the Frenchman's defection to Manchester United. John Lukic was also under fire following some indifferent performances. By the end of the first week of December, United were down to 15th with only one win in their last 10 games – a 3–0 home victory over Arsenal.

## Relegation battle

The champions were looking more like chumps as rebellion wrecked their stability. The irresistible force of the previous season was now proving cannon-fodder for the likes of Nottingham Forest – 4–1 winners at Elland Road! Rocastle enjoyed a little run, sharing in the 3–1 derby defeat of Sheffield Wednesday, but the most damning accusation of all was that Leeds were "quitters", that they were not working or fighting for their title.

A debut goal from Frank Strandli and an outstanding performance from Gary Speed were the highlights of the 3–0 revenge victory over Middlesbrough. The six-foot Norwegian forward had been brought on as a substitute just days after a £250,000 transfer from IK Start, and was seen as a likely replacement for the maturing Chapman. But he never really came to terms with the physical demands of the English game and eventually returned home.

By mid-February Leeds were being tipped for relegation, but fanciful talk of United becoming the first champions to be relegated since Manchester City some 50-odd years earlier was quickly dispelled. In the final analysis a wretched away record, which produced not a single victory and just seven points, could be seen as the deciding factor in what was truly a disappointing chapter. United finished 17th, the final joust giving Wilkinson some comfort as United battled back from 3–1 down to draw 3–3 at Coventry, courtesy of a fine Rod Wallace hat-trick.

# *1993–94*

Determined not to endure another winter of discontent, manager Wilkinson made some sweeping changes in the summer of 1993. Perhaps some of the players had approached the previous season in an over-confident state of mind. Certainly they had not worked enough on the field. Significantly, he reintroduced stamina training to the pre-season build-up and, acknowledging the need for changes, released ageing top-shot Lee Chapman and signed Sheffield United hit-man Brian Deane.

The season opened at Maine Road, where the Peacocks displayed all their true grit and colours to come away with a morale-boosting 1–1 draw. Leeds paraded many old favourites; Lukic in goal, Dorigo and Fairclough in defence, Batty, Strachan and McAllister in midfield and Speed up-front.

There were also, however, some interesting newcomers. Young Gary Kelly, promoted into the side, was an instant success at right-back. The Irish teenager was a particularly important find because United had not acquired a suitable replacement for the injured Mel Sterland and had spent much of the 1992–93 season without a recognized right-back, which naturally affected the balance of the team. Wilkinson spotted something in Kelly's play that persuaded him to convert him from his normal forward role. Whatever it was, it proved a winner.

**Jon Newsome's reputation grew with this goal in October 1993's 3–3 draw with Blackburn Rovers**

Brian Deane cost mega-bucks and arrived with a glowing testimony of goals for Sheffield United, a pedigree which seemed destined to continue when he made a scoring debut. But his integration into the Leeds fold was much more painful, and it was to take time before he settled in. He proved a durable character nonetheless, missing just one Premier League game and finishing the season as the second-from-top scorer with 11 goals.

Noel Whelan was given his chance as Deane's attacking partner, while at the heart of the defence Arsenal legend David O'Leary had been drafted in on a free transfer. He put on an "outstanding display" (Howard Wilkinson's description) but was injured two games later and made a very limited contribution to the season.

O'Leary's place was eventually shared between David Wetherall and Jon Newsome, and after three successive defeats at the hands of Norwich, Arsenal and Liverpool, a further change saw Mark Beeney take over from Lukic in goal.

## An away win

11 September 1993 produced a 2–0 win at Southampton; a significant psychological breakthrough, being Leeds' first away League win since April 1992! This hurdle cleared, United reeled off five straight wins, during which just one goal was conceded, and confidence grew as the unbeaten run stretched to 14 games.

One of football's most endearing features is its ability to switch from adversity to a state of optimism and fulfilment almost unnoticed; and when Leeds United entered 1994 in fourth position, following a 0–0 draw at Old Trafford, the credibility of Howard Wilkinson's team was fully restored.

Any thoughts of hustling the Reds for the title were dismissed by Manchester United's 15-point lead over their Yorkshire rivals, but qualification for a UEFA Cup slot was well within reach despite a run of six games without a win. "Hot Rod"'s 10 goals – he was to finish the season as leading scorer with 17 – was one of the reasons for the turn-round in fortunes, Wallace having been given a central striking role by the gaffer, who got him to sign a new four-year contract reported to be worth £800,000.

United wrapped up the season with a flourish, beating Swindon Town 5–0 at the County Ground –

**Tony Dorigo leaves Manchester United's Roy Keane for dead during a goalless draw at Old Trafford**

the fifth goal by Chris Fairclough being the 100th conceded in the FA Carling Premiership by Swindon that season. United were fifth and in the UEFA Cup. What a difference a year makes.

# *1994–95*

United breezed into Upton Park looking for a fourth successive win in the tight East London stadium and hoping that Brian Deane would improve on a record of scoring in the last six opening-day games. The close season had seen some frantic activity in the transfer market, with England midfielder Carlton Palmer now on the payroll after a £2.8 million switch from Sheffield Wednesday, while Jon Newsome had joined Norwich City in a £1 million deal.

Palmer, recruited to fill the void left by Batty, was in the starting-line at West Ham but Tomas Skuhravy was not, a £3 million deal having collapsed after a last-minute hitch developed between the Czech striker and his club Genoa. It was a pity, as Leeds desperately needed a ruthless edge to their attack. Deane failed to extend his record and the closest anyone came to a goal was when Rod Wallace broke through, only to be grounded by a blatant professional foul by Alvin Martin.

Northern Ireland international Nigel Worthington had made his debut at left-back, after rejecting new terms from Sheffield Wednesday, and was to maintain

**Noel Whelan beats Arsenal's David Seaman to net United's first goal of the 1994–95 campaign**

YEBOAH

an almost constant presence in defence until the end of February. For the opening home game against Arsenal, South African striker Philomen Masinga, who had made his debut as a sub at West Ham, took over from the injured Deane.

It was young Noel Whelan who stole the goalscoring prize, however, netting the only goal against the Gunners and hitting the target again in the next two fixtures against Chelsea (lost 2–3) and Crystal Palace (won 2–1). He added two more in the 2–0 defeat of Manchester City to take his tally to four in five starts and two subtitute appearances, and continued to make the headlines with the winner against Leicester City. United had twice been denied by the woodwork in this one, but were in luck the third time when Whelan's header went in off the underside of the crossbar. Skipper Gary McAllister had produced a sweet opener, and although United were ninth, 11 points adrift of Premiership leaders Newcastle, they were looking more like a team with an interest in the championship.

## Yeboah's arrival

It would be premature to claim that Wilkinson had hit on a title-winning blend, since Gordon Strachan, restricted by a troublesome back, had virtually retired as a player after the opening week, while the cutting edge up-front remained inconsistent. Little Rod Wallace destroyed his former club Southampton at the Dell with two goals but was not to score again for five months, while Deane had a dry run of 10 games and Masinga finished the season with figures of five goals in 15 (7) games. It was not until the introduction of Yeboah in mid-February that Leeds began to carry the punch of champions.

The Ghanaian powerhouse had finally received his work permit clearance on 19 January, and quickly completed a £3.4 million transfer from Eintracht Frankfurt. Substitute appearances against QPR and Blackburn were followed by a scoring full debut against Everton (1–0). He showed his class to the full at Filbert Street, where Leicester were outplayed comprehensively. Yeboah scored two and paved the way for Palmer to run through unchallenged for a third. That made it six goals in nine appearances, four as substitute, and took him to within a goal of joint top scorers Brian Deane and Noel Whelan. Yeboah would finish the season with 13 goals in 17 games, the main reason for the club's strong finish.

**Leeds' Ghanaian powerhouse, striker Tony Yeboah, proves you can't keep a good man down**

With 33 games played Leeds were sixth, just below Liverpool, with Blackburn Rovers 24 points ahead in pole position. The championship was well out of reach but United could still qualify for Europe and influence the outcome of the title race.

The defection of Gordon Strachan to Coventry City in March was another shock. The wee man, while not contributing on the field, was still a very influential and inspiring individual on Wilkinson's right hand and there is no doubt his departure was sadly accepted. It was public knowledge that he was being groomed as Wilkinson's successor, but Ron Atkinson, in trouble at Highfield Road, promised the Scot almost immediate hands-on control of Coventry City and he jumped at the chance. But United continued to grind out results, with McAllister and Palmer the keystones in the middle of a potentially successful combination.

They looked a good bet for Europe thanks to a 30th-minute goal from Brian Deane at Liverpool, though it needed two outstanding saves from John Lukic – ever-present this season – to ensure Leeds' first victory at Anfield for 23 years. His first, a spectacular reflex save, deflected Fowler's fierce drive over the bar; for the second he got a hand to Kennedy's scorching 25-yarder to divert the ball on to the crossbar.

Brian Deane then threw Alex Ferguson a title lifeline with a dramatic last-gasp goal, 87 seconds into injury time, for a 1–1 draw at Ewood Park; yet impressive as this was, United went into the final day of the season needing a point at Tottenham to stay in the top five and guarantee European football for West Yorkshire. It didn't look good when Sheringham volleyed Spurs ahead on the half-hour and a super demonstration of goalkeeping from Ian Walker thwarted Yeboah. But he could not stop Brian Deane in the 67th minute; the gangly striker ran half the length of the pitch and held off two defenders before steering an angled left-foot shot into the net for a well-deserved 1–1 draw.

United were in Europe: just reward for Wilkinson, who only a couple of weeks before had turned down a £3 million fortune to manage Turkish giants Galatasaray. He said: "When you compare what I am earning here with what I could have picked up by joining Galatasaray, you could say I have invested millions in Leeds United. I think that is a testimony to my commitment, dedication and loyalty to the job still to be done at Elland Road."

**Tony Yeboah scores again, this time against Chelsea, on November 18, 1995**

# 1995–96

In many ways, the 1995–96 season had to be considered a success. After all, when a team has failed to grace a Cup Final for over 20 years a Wembley appearance, even if it is a defeat, must be a positive improvement. However, if any Leeds fan were to be asked about that season, he would reply with a shake of the head and murmurs of disappointment.

Leeds got off to a flying start with consecutive victories over West Ham away and Liverpool and Aston Villa at home, going top of the table with maximum points. Two weeks later, Monaco came to Yorkshire for a UEFA Cup tie and left with their tails between their legs after a comprehensive 3–0 thrashing that effectively rendered the second leg almost meaningless.

These results were conclusive enough. Yet the performances were not entirely convincing: there was an air of uncertainty, even of brittleness, about United's appearances. So perhaps it was not too surprising when things somehow began to unravel. QPR strolled to a 3–1 victory at Elland Road, David Wetherall's 89th-minute goal scant consolation in a shock defeat; then Notts County from Division Two comfortably held their own in the Coca-Cola Cup, with a potentially tricky second leg at Meadow Lane to come.

## Dutch masters

Leeds' hopes of success in European competition were unceremoniously brought to an end as PSV Eindhoven destroyed them 5–3 at Elland Road, and 3–0 in the second leg. The tie was effectively over by half-time in the first leg as the Dutchmen, counter-attacking brilliantly, scored three times. This was the third time in only 31 days that United had conceded three goals at home.

Tony Yeboah's 80th-minute goal was enough to beat Chelsea and lift Leeds back up to fourth place in the Premiership, but it was the last time United were in the top half-dozen in the table.

A defeat against Newcastle in the next game saw Leeds drop to eighth, and the decline was even more apparent. A brief glimmer of hope came around Christmas with consecutive victories over Manchester United (3–1) and Bolton (2–0), but the festive cheer didn't last.

**Brian Deane scores one against Southampton in the 1995–96 season**

### Wembley run a distraction

The Coca-Cola Cup offered a small glimpse of relief in the season and defeats of Blackburn and Reading earned Leeds a semi-final berth. However, preparations for the Birmingham tie could hardly have gone worse as Liverpool (5–0), Nottingham Forest (2–1) and Aston Villa (3–0) all enjoyed comfortable home victories over the men from Elland Road. The Premiership losing run – after the Coca-Cola Cup Final and FA Cup quarter-final were reached – continued unabated with a 1–0 defeat by almost-doomed Bolton Wanderers.

On 6 March, two Tony Yeboah goals in the opening 25 minutes were enough to see off Queens Park Rangers at Loftus Road, but it was to be Leeds' penultimate victory of the season. They were now stuck in the bottom half of the table, and preparations for the Coca-Cola Cup Final continued to go badly.

### Long losing run

After Aston Villa had comprehensively outplayed United at Wembley, Leeds lost to a fourth-minute penalty at home to Middlesbrough but bounced back after a fashion, Brian Deane's goal being enough to beat Southampton at Elland Road. As injuries and a lack of confidence took an even stronger hold, things went from bad to worse: six straight defeats followed.

This sequence equalled the club record for most consecutive defeats in the League and only the good early-season form meant that relegation was not an issue. The final-day draw at Coventry stopped the rot (defeat would have condemned the Midlanders to the drop), but the most telling statistic of a disappointing campaign was that only bottom-of-the-table Bolton Wanderers lost more than Leeds' eight home games.

## *1996–97*

The summer of 1996 had been a time for change. Wilkinson had stopped looking like the spectre at the feast and begun to tuck in as he enticed an exciting array of talent to Elland Road, including Nigel Martyn, arriving from Crystal Palace; Ian Rush, on a free from Liverpool; Lee Bowyer, a £2.6 million signing from Charlton Athletic; and Manchester United's Lee Sharpe. The new boys appeared by kind permission of the club's new owners, the Caspian Group, who provided a welcome cash injection. Given the elbow or leaving of their own accord were Speed, who departed for Everton, McAllister (Coventry City), Lukic (Arsenal) and Worthington (Stoke City).

Perhaps Yeboah would inspire his colleagues to greatness. He and Rush certainly constituted the oldest strikers in town, but the prospect of them coming together encouraged visions of spectacle. It wasn't to be, however. Injuries and international engagements restricted Yeboah to less than a handful of games, while Rush, willing and committed, could not roll back the years as he endured the longest goal-drought of his career. Brolin, clearly phased by the physical requirements of the English game, went walk-about in Europe and Sharpe likewise proved a great disappointment, despite scoring some fine goals.

There was disquiet in the camp, and Wilkinson – the man who had masterminded the second great era of Leeds United – was axed on 9 September, his departure hastened by a supporters' backlash in the wake of a 4–0 home defeat by great rivals Manchester United. George Graham, who had revived the fortunes of Arsenal, was immediately appointed as his replacement but could not inspire an instant response.

### George Graham's arrival

Graham inherited a talented squad suffering an injury crisis. Front-line strikers Deane and Yeboah were long-term absentees and the Swede Tomas Brolin had gone to Zurich. However, new goalkeeper Martyn was a revelation – so good, in fact, that he won his way back into the England squad – and Leeds became a difficult side to beat: indeed, they conceded only a single goal at home in 1997, ending the campaign in 11th place.

What was required, more than ever, was star quality; players who could fill Elland Road and restore confidence and pride in the club through quality and consistency. Leeds needed a bit of swank and swagger; not loud-mouthed immodesty, but the kind of justifiable professional assurance which meant Don Revie could wake up on a Saturday morning and say, "I'd hate to be playing us today."

You'd know what I mean if you'd ever seen Giles and Bremner orchestrating when United were in their pomp, or "Sniffer" Clarke homing in on goal. It's what Strachan gave to Leeds before his back gave out. There was a time when all top-class sides possessed such quality, but it's a rare commodity nowadays.

### Elland Road a fortress again

It wasn't until Rush scored twice, in a 3–0 victory over Leicester City in January, that the team began to take shape. It ended a dreadful run of six games without a

**Rod Wallace (left) celebrates his goal against Forest with Mark Ford and Lee Sharpe (right)**

win during which just one strike, from Deane, had been registered. The irony was that Rush, suffering his worst run of form ever – one goal in 22 games – had offered to stand down to give others a chance. But Graham declined – and was thankful he had.

The new boss predictably started building his team from the back, and with goalkeeper Nigel Martyn in the sort of form that won him a deserved recall to the England international squad as well as the supporters' Player of the Year trophy, United emerged in the second half of the season as one of the hardest teams to beat in the FA Carling Premiership. Radebe, Halle, Molenaar and Harte played their parts, and the only disappointment was John Scales who reneged on an agreement to join United from Liverpool by going off and playing for Spurs instead.

Leeds finished 11th, after a climatic finale against a Middlesbrough side needing a win to stay up. Brian Deane killed them off in a 1–1 draw; and hardly had the showers run cold than George Graham was busy, eager to make peace with unsettled strike pair Brolin and Yeboah.

In summer 1997, Leeds went to market. A cheque for £3.25 million eventually persuaded Crystal Palace to part with midfield ball-winner David Hopkin and United also secured the services of Jimmy Floyd Hasselbaink (£2 million from Boavista), Alf Inge Haaland (a tribunal-set £1.6 million from Nottingham Forest), Bruno Ribeiro (£500,000 from Vitoria Setubal) and Rangers' David Robertson (another £500,000).

Out went Brian Deane (£1.5 million to Sheffield United), Mark Ford, who went to Burnley for £250,000), Andy Couzens (to Carlisle United for £100,000) and Lawrence Davies and John Pemberton, who joined Bradford City and Crewe respectively on free transfers.

# Chapter 3

# Leeds in Europe

**Jet travel and television have shrunk the sporting world and added a new dimension to the football calendar. Leeds, the last winners of the Inter-Cities Fairs Cup and finalists in three major European club competitions, have done much to establish England's Continental credentials.**

## *The shame of Paris*

Perhaps Leeds' finest achievement on the Continent came in 1975. Jimmy Armfield had guided United to impressive victories over Anderlecht and Barcelona to reach the European Champions' Cup Final. The style of those triumphs in the earlier rounds gained Leeds worldwide respect, and though their final opponents in Paris were Franz Beckenbauer's Bayern Munich the Yorkshiremen were fancied to claim Europe's most coveted club prize. So Wednesday 28 May 1975 was set to be the proudest moment in Leeds United's history. Instead, events on and off the field were to leave a bitter taste in the mouth.

Leeds conducted themselves impeccably on the field. Paul Madeley replaced the suspended Gordon McQueen at centre-half and with Billy Bremner taking the initiative alongside Johnny Giles and Terry Yorath in midfield Bayern found themselves chasing the ball.

Smooth, gilt-edged passing, creative running off the ball and as always that stubborn resolute defence left the Germans second-best during a first half in which Leeds not only should have taken the lead but deserved to. During the opening half-hour goalkeeper Dave Stewart handled the ball only twice.

Midway through the first period, a Leeds attack created an opening for Allan Clarke. The England striker had his foot cocked, ready to hammer the ball at goal, when his legs were whipped from under him by a desperate challenge from Beckenbauer. Everyone, including Bayern fans, knew it was a penalty; everyone, that is, apart from the referee, M. Kitabdjian.

Despite the anguish, the disappointment, frustration and injustice of being denied their rights, and another dismissed penalty claim, the players kept their cool and their composure to continue to chip away at the fortunate Bayern defence. They even accepted the referee's decision to disallow a spectacular goal by Peter Lorimer in the 66th minute.

## *The winner that wasn't*

Lorimer was some 12 yards out when he unleashed a thunderous volley that would have taken Georg Schwarzenbeck's head off had he not ducked. The ball whistled into the top corner of Sepp Maier's net before the 'keeper could flex a muscle. It was a wonderful goal, worthy of winning any cup final.

But not this one. M. Kitabdjian ruled that Bremner was offside – and perhaps he was by a fraction, for he was level with Durnberger on the six-yard line – but he was not interfering with play. Maier was well and truly beaten by Lorimer's right-footed blast.

Yorath never stopped prompting from midfield. A 30-yarder from Norman Hunter rattled the bar; Lorimer shot just wide; Maier somewhat fortunately blocked Bremner's effort from point-blank range. There was a feeling that it was not going to be Leeds' night.

Armfield's men had controlled the game, but then Bayern got more lucky breaks. Dieter Roth clipped an inch-perfect shot past the advancing Stewart to steal the lead in the 72nd minute, and Gerd Müller put the game beyond reach when he poached a second 10 minutes later, getting goalside of Madeley to turn Horst Kapellmann's cross in at the near post.

The misbehaviour of a section of the Leeds support earned their club a ban from European competition. Yet amid the blazing emotion and the torrid scenes which pulsated in Paris that night, Bremner and his team put on a football show which was possibly the finest by any Leeds side in Europe.

# *The final countdown*

The road to Paris had started at Elland Road some eight months earlier, when Swiss champions FC Zurich were clinically dispatched 4–1. Allan Clarke claimed two goals, Lorimer struck from the penalty spot and fearsome Joe Jordan netted his first European Cup goal. Clarke was on the scoresheet again in the second leg, which was lost 2–1, but the 5–3 aggregate victory was comprehensive enough. United's domestic form was not matching their exploits abroad, so a 2–1 lead taken in the first leg at Ujpest Dozsa lifted morale.

Lorimer scored this time from open play while giant defender McQueen made the most of his physique to force the winner. Indeed, the Hungarians found the big Scot intimidating and he opened the scoring in the second leg. Bremner and Yorath added further goals for a 3–0 victory and a 5–1 aggregate passage into the quarter-final.

**SO CLOSE AGAIN**

**European Champions Cup Final**

**28 May 1975**
Parc des Princes, Paris – Attendance: 48,000

**Leeds United 0**
**Bayern Munich 2**

**Team:** Harvey, Reaney, F. Gray, Bremner, Madeley, Hunter, Lorimer, Clarke, Jordan, Giles, Yorath (E. Gray)

Paired with Anderlecht, the fans were in for a treat, with two classic games securing Leeds a 4–0 aggregate victory. The tie was effectively won in the first leg at home, where Jordan and McQueen's power in the air proved decisive. A goal each from them and an unstoppable third from Lorimer thrilled the 43,195 crowd. Bremner notched the winner in Belgium to set up a semi-final showdown with mighty Barcelona.

# *Cruyff and Co.*

The first leg, at home, was crucial. Armfield was anxious to keep a clean sheet and knew he had to tie down the Dutch masters Johan Cruyff and Johann Neeskens. The game was tense and nervy – it was the 60th competitive match of the season for United – but Bremner and Giles were full of running and determined to master the midfield battle.

**Leeds score against the mighty Barcelona side that included Johan Cruyff and Johann Neeskens**

Little Billy eased the tension with a brilliant goal in the ninth minute. Giles played the ball up to Jordan who headed on for Bremner, and he took it in his stride before thumping an angled shot past Salvador Sadurni. It was the first goal to have been conceded by the Spaniards in Europe that season, and they were visibly shocked.

Armfield was hoping for a two-goal cushion to take

**Leeds managed to put 16 goals past Lyn Oslo over two legs**

to the Nou Camp, and Clarke and McQueen went close with headers. Madeley was doing a grand job shadowing Cruyff, but the pace of the Spanish on the break was always a threat, and in the 66th minute the pendulum swung Barcelona's way when a clinical pass from Cruyff found Juan Carlos Heredia.

Paul Reaney's challenge on the edge of the box seemed fair enough but a free kick was given against the full-back. Cruyff took charge, taking his time before rolling the ball short to Asensi, whose shot swerved beyond Stewart: 1–1!

Barcelona now had one foot in the final and the odds on their side, but you could not discount the fighting quality of this Leeds line-up.

With 12 minutes to go Reaney surged down the right; his cross was perfect, Jordan headed it down and "Sniffer" Clarke swooped to deliver one of his classical strikes from six yards and net his 21st goal of the season.

Even so, Barcelona remained firm favourites, but Lorimer took the wind out of their sails with an early strike in Spain. The temperature got hotter, the tackles tougher, and McQueen was shown the red card. But 10-man United battled heroically to hang on for a 1–1 draw and clinch their first European Cup Final place on a 3–2 aggregate.

United had come close to making the final in 1969–70 when the first European Cup tie at Elland Road provided a goal bonanza. Lyn Oslo were beaten 10–0, a United record – one better than the 9–0 drubbing of Spora (Luxembourg) in the Fairs Cup two years previously.

So Leeds joined three other clubs who had scored 10: Manchester United, Ipswich and Benfica. It had taken just 40 seconds to open the account, with Mike O'Grady, unsettled and the subject of an £80,000 bid from Wolves, sweeping in from the left to latch on to Madeley's pass inside the back and finish with a textbook angled shot from 18 yards.

Poor Svein Olsen, a colourful but erratic goalkeeper, could do little to halt the goal feast as Mick Jones hit three, Clarke, Giles and Bremner two each.

# Goals galore

The Norwegian champions were hit for six more in Oslo, the 16–0 aggregate a new English record, overtaking Ipswich Town's 14–0 demolition of Maltese outfit Floriana in 1962 but two short of Benfica's 18–0 record. And this was achieved in spite of the absence of Charlton, Giles, Clarke and Hunter, all under treatment at home.

Jones scored four, Giles and Lorimer one each in the 6–0 aggregate win over Hungarians Ferencvaros in round two, while Lorimer's 71st-minute strike left Standard Liège reeling in another European supershow from United.

The Belgians were comprehensively beaten by some stunning, well-controlled, almost faultless football, and in the home leg Liège were destroyed with the clinical power of a waste-disposal unit. Another goal – this time a Giles penalty – another clean sheet and a 2–0 aggregate victory.

Leeds were favourites for the semi-final with Celtic, billed as the "Battle of Britain". But embroiled in the chase for three titles United came unstuck, and after losing 1–0 to the Scots in the first leg just could not find the reserves of strength required to overturn the result at Celtic Park. Bremner scored but it wasn't enough. Celtic won through to the European Cup Final 3–1.

# A second chance

After winning the League Championship in 1992 Leeds were back in the Champions' Cup, and their 1992–93 campaign opened with huge controversy. Though a 3–0 defeat in Stuttgart left Howard Wilkinson's team with a mountain to climb they met the challenge in a pulsating second leg, with one each from Gary Speed, Gary McAllister, Eric Cantona and Lee Chapman. But Andreas Buck had scored for Stuggart to make the result 4–1 on the night and 4–4 on aggregate: enough, it seemed, to provide the Germans with a passport into the second round on the away goals rule.

However, it was soon noticed that one of Stuttgart's substitutes was not a German national. UEFA rules at the time allowed for only three non-nationals to be named in any squad, and although there were never more than three on the pitch during the match the rule

**Eric Cantona takes the ball past Stuttgart's Fritz Walter in October 1992**

had been contravened, because one non-German replaced another. UEFA gave the game to Leeds with a 3–0 scoreline, meaning a 3–3 aggregate, and ordered a third match to be played, but decided to stage it at Barcelona. At such short notice just 7,400 fans made it to the 110,000-capacity stadium to witness Leeds' 2–1 victory, the scorers being Gordon Strachan, playing one of the games of his life, and Carl Shutt.

A 2–1 defeat at Glasgow Rangers did not seem an insurmountable obstacle to address in the return game, McAllister's goal keeping Leeds in the hunt, but on the night United just could not get into top gear. Although Cantona was on target again Rangers repeated their 2–1 win to eliminate the English champions 4–2, and end United's dreams of a lucrative place in the round-robin Champions' League phase.

## *First among equals*

The European Cup, of course, is the Holy Grail for the Continent's finest, and Wednesday 29 September 1965 saw another landmark in the history of Leeds United with the arrival at Elland Road of Torino for United's first-ever competitive match in Europe.

You have to be in English soccer's élite to have a chance of Continental competition, and three years prior to this engagement such opportunities had seemed beyond United's dreams.

Revie had built his team around Bobby Collins, and on this damp, warm Yorkshire night the little genius pulled all the strings. It was a memorable night as, inspired by young Bremner, Leeds defeated the Italians 2–1. It could have been more: United should have had four or five in the first half.

**Leeds dispatched Torino in the 1965–66 European Cup campaign – their first in Europe**

The manager sent out his forwards in differently-numbered shirts and positions from those usually adopted, in order to confuse Torino's man-to-man marking policy; but it was their goalkeeper, Vieri, and centre-half Puja who caught the eye as Leeds launched their offensive.

United's first European goal was claimed by Bremner in the 25th minute, a touchline shot which exploded off the goalkeeper's shoulder into the far corner. Alan Peacock, followed everywhere by two leech-like defenders, did superbly well to head home a second, but as United pressed for a third Orlando stole away on the right and, using two decoys, cleverly pushed home the Italian reply.

The United team on that historic night was: Sprake; Reaney, Madeley, Bremner, Charlton, Hunter, Giles, Lorimer, Peacock, Collins and Cooper.

The return game was to prove costly. A bad foul by Poletti left Collins with a fractured right thigh, but despite being down to 10 men for 40 minutes Leeds showed the character of champions to force a goalless draw. Revie's renowned defence surpassed themselves. The half-back line had possibly its finest hour. Big Jack held the middle from the first minute and Bremner and Hunter covered acres on their flanks; challenging, intercepting, hustling and pressuring their adversaries to part with the ball.

No less an authority than Vittorio Pozzo, Italy's World Cup manager in 1934 and 1938, watched in admiration. He said: "This was the fastest game for a long time in Italy. Leeds are a robust, determined team, full of willpower and with exceptional ability.

"This team had said a word about British soccer which for years had not been heard and which convinced the crowd. The whole team seemed to be spurred by fire, but the work performed by inside-left Collins and right-half Bremner will not be forgotten soon by those who watched the game."

Lorimer and Bremner scored in a 2–1 win at SC Leipzig, but there was no score in the home tie. A torrid 1–1 draw with Valencia at Elland Road was hardly a good advert for the game. The match was fiery from the start and erupted into a players' brawl. Dutch referee Leo Horn, an official with a good reputation, lost it this day. He sent three off, Jack Charlton and full-back Videgan for fighting and Lage for a foul on Storrie. Munoz fired the Spaniards into a 16th-minute lead but Lorimer's whiplash volley from a cross by Giles brought Leeds level.

Revie protested as Valencia waged war, but he had the last laugh when, after 75 minutes of the second leg, a great goal by Mike O'Grady kept United among the heads of European football, when he shrugged off a double tackle and tucked the ball away from an angle.

So Leeds were into the last eight in their first-ever European competition and Ujpest Dozsa were swept away 5–2 on aggregate, the triumph sparked by a rare Euro goal from Terry Cooper.

## *The real thing*

The semi-final provided a much sterner test as United faced Spanish opposition again. Real Zaragoza won 1–0 on home soil but Leeds hit back with a 2–1 victory, Albert Johanneson and Charlton the marksmen. It stood 2–2 on aggregate and, when Leeds won the toss for choice of replay venue, dreams of a final were rampant. But the Spanish were a class outfit and took the breath away as they stormed into a three-goal lead inside 13 minutes. Jack Charlton clawed one back but Leeds never got near them.

Still, Yorkshire's appetite for European football had been whetted and United's continued presence in the Inter-Cities Fairs Cup was well-received. The 1966–67 attempt was even more gratifying, for overcoming DWS Amsterdam (8–2 agg.), Valencia (3–1 agg.), Bologna (on the toss of a coin following a 1–1 draw on aggregate) and Kilmarnock (4–2 agg.) they reached the final against Dinamo Zagreb.

The trip to Yugoslavia was spoiled by the absences through injury of Giles, Bell, Madeley and Johanneson, their places being taken by Bates, Belfitt, Eddie Gray and O'Grady. Revie erred on the side of caution and tried to contain the Yugoslavs, but once Sprake was beaten by a thumping header from 18-year-old reserve winger Cercek, Charlton pushed up to lend nuisance value to the attack. O'Grady and Hunter's efforts might have brought rewards but Zagreb were in the driving seat, and when skipper Zambata turned on some dazzling magic to set up Rora to score Leeds could only try to limit the damage.

The big worry for Revie in the second leg was a scoring drought. Peacock had hardly featured since February 1966, though the manager did think of giving him a go, but decided against it. There was one surprise, however, as Willie Bell came in at full-back while Reaney moved on to the wing.

Fired up and eager to please, United put the Zagreb goal under siege, but acrobatic goalkeeping brilliance from Skoric, some wayward finishing and a huge slice of luck all combined to deny Leeds.

Jimmy Greenhoff might have scored with a header; Charlton and Belfitt had chances disallowed and Bremner's best effort was hacked away from under the crossbar. It all added up to a 0–0 draw and Yugoslavia's title.

**FIRST FINAL**

**European Fairs Cup Final**

| 1st leg **30 August 1967** | 2nd leg **7 September 1967** |
|---|---|
| Dinamo Stadium, Zagreb | Elland Road, Leeds |
| Attendance: 40,000 | Attendance: 35,000 |
| **Dinamo Zagreb 2** | **Leeds United 0** |
| **Leeds United 0** | **Dinamo Zagreb 0** |
| **Team:** Sprake, Reaney, Cooper, Bremner, Charlton, Hunter, Bates, Lorimer, Belfitt, E Gray, O'Grady | **Team:** Sprake, Bell, Cooper, Bremner, Charlton, Hunter, Reaney, Belfitt, Greenhoff, Giles, O'Grady |

## *Sweet success*

Still, they say the experience of failure makes you appreciate success even more, and no triumph was sweeter than the one over Ferencvaros in 1968.

United disposed of Spora Luxembourg 16–0 on aggregate, Lorimer hitting four in the first leg (9–0) and Johanneson three in the second. A trip to Yugoslavia proved more fruitful this time around as Partizan of Belgrade went down 3–2 after United won the away leg 2–1. It was to prove Leeds' final trip outside of Britain until the final, as the opposition in the next three rounds were all from north of the border. In the third round Hibernian went down 2–1; it was Rangers who were overcome in the quarter-final 2–0, and Dundee were brushed aside in the semi-final 2–1 on aggregate. Each of the three games followed a similar pattern, with Leeds winning the home leg and getting a draw in Scotland.

Leeds enjoyed the comfort of home for the first leg of the final in which the Hungarians played it hard and tight, looking, as always, to hit on the break. They might have taken the lead when Charlton lost concentration and let in Szoke, while at the other end 'keeper

**United defeated Italian giants Juventus – albeit on the away goals rule – to bring home the Inter-Cities Fairs Cup in 1971: they were the last team to win it**

| **European CHAMPS** | **European Fairs Cup Final** |
|---|---|
| 1st leg **7 September 1968** | 2nd leg **11 September 1968** |
| Elland Road, Leeds | Nep Stadium, Budapest |
| Attendance: 25,000 | Attendance: 25,000 |
| **Leeds United 1** (Jones) | **Ferencvaros 0** |
| **Ferencvaros 0** | **Leeds United 0** |
| **Team:** Sprake, Reaney, Cooper, Bremner, Charlton, Hunter, Lorimer, Madeley, Jones (Belfitt), Giles (Greenhoff), E. Gray | **Team:** Sprake, Reaney, Cooper, Bremner, Charlton, Hunter, O'Grady, Lorimer, Jones, Madeley, Hibbitt (Bates) |

Geczi made amends, after misplacing a goalkick to Jones, by saving Lorimer's final shot.

The crucial goal came from a Lorimer corner in the 40th minute. Charlton, standing right in front of the 'keeper beneath the bar, stood his ground amid the jostling to head down and Mick Jones bundled the ball over the line. A scrappy goal, but one that was to win the Inter-Cities Fairs Cup, for though it seemed a very slim advantage to take to Hungary, Sprake was in top form and the 10-man defence held fast.

# A fair test

Leeds were to win the Fairs Cup again in 1971. It came as some consolation after they had just conceded the League championship to Arsenal in the last stride.

But it was a tough competition, for Leeds had to overcome Sarpsborg (6–0 agg), Dynamo Dresden (2–2: won on away goals), Sparta Prague (9–2 agg), Vitoria Setubal (3–2 agg) and, in the semi-final, Liverpool. A Bremner goal at Anfield saw them through to a money-spinning final with Juventus.

| **Second SUCCESS** | **Inter-Cities Fairs Cup Final** |
|---|---|
| 1st leg **28 May 1971** | 2nd leg **3 June 1971** |
| Communale, Turin | White Hart Lane, Tottenham |
| Attendance: 65,000 | Attendance: 42,000 |
| **Juventus 2** | **Leeds United 1** (Clarke) |
| **Leeds United 2** (Madeley, Bates) | **Juventus 1** |
| **Team:** Sprake: Reaney, Cooper, Bremner, Charlton, Hunter, Lorimer, Clarke, Jones (Bates), Giles, Madeley | **Team:** Sprake: Reaney, Cooper, Bremner, Charlton, Hunter, Lorimer, Clarke, Jones, Giles, Madeley (Bates) |

A 1–1 draw in the second leg at Elland Road was enough to overcome the Italian giants. Pietro Anastasi had equalized Clarke's early goal to make the aggregate score 3–3 but the two goals Leeds scored in Turin through Madeley and substitute Mick Bates, after Juventus had twice taken the lead, secured Leeds the trophy under the away goals rule.

Clarke's 11th-minute strike, a low right-footed shot after Lorimer had failed to connect with Bremner's floated free kick, was the kind of start they needed.

The Italians, sharp and decisive on the break, were level after 18 minutes when Anastasi took advantage of a hopeless tangle in the Leeds defence to roll the ball past Sprake from close range.

Roberto Tancredi, who had replaced the anxious Piloni in goal, saved well from Lorimer and Giles but was relieved when Clarke's drive veered just wide of the far post. He was extended to the full right before the break, just managing to tip over a solid header from Jones.

The Italians, too, had their moments but Sprake remained cool and safe under pressure and in the dying embers of the final, when Juve made a desperate attempt to snatch victory from the jaws of defeat, the Welsh custodian did Leeds proud with a full-length save from Giuseppe Furino.

# End of an era

Thus Leeds United became the last club to win the Fairs Cup, for the following season UEFA assumed control of a competition which had such humble beginnings hardly anyone noticed it. But this was the forerunner of the UEFA Cup.

As defending Fairs Cup-holders, Leeds took their place in the inaugural UEFA Cup but went out in their first tie, 4–2 on aggregate to SK Lierse. The result was a huge surprise after goals from Galvin and Lorimer had given United a 2–0 victory in the first leg. The side which travelled to Belgium was lacking many first-teamers and it was not strong enough, the final score being 4–0 to SK Lierse.

Leeds did have another chance of winning a trophy in Europe that season when, as the last holders of the

Fairs Cup, they played Barcelona, the first winners, to decide who would keep the trophy permanently.

The game was staged at the Nou Camp, Barcelona, in September 1971, and though Joe Jordan scored for United the Spaniards managed two goals of their own to ensure that the silverware remained in the Catalan club's trophy cabinet.

Since then United's involvement in the UEFA Cup has been brief. They were knocked out in the third round in 1973–74 by Vitoria Setubal from Portugal (2–3 on aggregate), after a comfortable win over Norwegians Stromgodset (7–2 on aggregate) and a tough battle with Scotland's Hibernian (0–0 on aggregate, 5–4 on penalties).

In the 1979–80 season Leeds' presence was even shorter-lived, for after a 7–0 aggregate win over Valetta of Malta the Romanians of Universitatea Craiova unceremoniously dumped United on their backs with two 2–0 victories.

## *Painful lesson*

The most recent foray into Europe involved Howard Wilkinson's side in the autumn of 1995. There was plenty of fun and games while it lasted, but it was not for too long.

In Monaco, fans were treated to compelling evidence of Tony Yeboah's scoring prowess as he hit all three to just about guarantee Leeds a place in the second round. The home tie was seen as a formality, but Monaco showed surprising grit by winning 1–0 at Elland Road – and it could have been worse but for a brilliant display by goalkeeper Lukic.

**Tony Yeboah (centre) scored three in the away match against Monaco in 1995**

**AC Milan put Leeds out of the Cup-Winners' Cup**

The European dream was turned into a nightmare in Round Two when PSV Eindhoven travelled to Elland Road and went home with a 5–3 victory. Leeds, who had struggled in the Premiership just before this tie, found the score 3–1 before too long had elapsed. United fought back very well to draw level at 3–3, but hadn't learned their lesson, and two goals in the final five minutes by Belgian international Luc Nilis sounded the death-knell for any real hopes of progress to the third round. It was not a good way for Leeds' 100th match in European competition to end.

PSV finished the job in Eindhoven, the 3–0 reverse leaving Wilkinson an angry man. John Pemberton, who gifted PSV their second with a 43rd-minute own goal, admitted: "We came here to salvage a bit of pride but simply didn't do ourselves justice. By the end it was men against boys."

## Cup-Winners' Cup

United have had only one tilt at the European Cup-Winners' Cup, and this was in 1972–73 when they went all the way to the final, conceding just three goals in nine ties.

The venture started in the unknown territory of Istanbul where, thanks to a Joe Jordan goal, a 1–1 draw with Ankaragucu was achieved. The Turkish cup-winners were certainly no pushovers and Leeds were somewhat relieved to scrape home 1–0, courtesy of a Mick Jones goal, at Elland Road.

Next to East Germany, where United's defensive mastery secured a goalless draw with Carl Zeiss Jena. Anther clean sheet in the home leg and goals from Jordan and Trevor Cherry wrapped it up.

Leeds were in the quarter-final, and drawn against Rapid Bucharest. The Romanians were just returning after their mid-winter break and were ruthlesssly exposed as Leeds romped to a 5–0 victory at Elland Road. Peter Lorimer hit the target twice; Clarke, Jordan and Giles completed the onslaught. The demoralised Romanians offered litltle resistance in the second leg which Leeds took 3–1, Jordan, Jones and Mick Bates hitting the target.

An Allan Clarke goal in the first leg of the semi-final against Hajduk Split was enough to see off the Yugoslav challenge and earn a final showdown with AC Milan in Salonica.

## Beware of Greeks bearing gifts

To say that Leeds were hardly in the right frame of mind to meet Milan is an understatement. The final came in the wake of the shock FA Cup Final defeat by second-division Sunderland at Wembley and, with rumours circulating that Don Revie was leaving the club to take over England, the atmosphere was very heavy.

Injuries to Jones (though he played) and to Giles, coupled with the suspensions of Clarke and Bremner, only intensified the feeling of gloom and despondency in the United camp – even the weather joined in on the act, thunder and heavy rain engulfing the new Kaftatzoglio Stadium.

And it didn't get any better – especially when the Greek referee Christos Michas penalised Madeley for a mysterious infringement after only four minutes .

The upshot was that Luciano Chiarugi's free kick clipped a United defender, came off a Milan body to deflect on to the foot of the post and spun in.

After that Milan withdrew into a defensive shell, repelling all Leeds' efforts by fair and foul means. Jones and Lorimer were flattened in the box and Romeo Benetti blatantly handled Paul Reaney's cross, but Michas ignored everything until Hunter reacted when felled from behind and the Leeds man was sent off with Sogliano.

**Greek TRAGEDY**

**European Cup-Winners' Cup Final**

**16 May 1973**
Kaftatzoglio Stadium, Salonica
Attendance: 45,000

**Inter Milan 1**
**Leeds United 0**

**Team:** Harvey, Reaney, Cherry, Bates, Madeley, Hunter, F. Gray (McQueen), Yorath, Lorimer, Jordan, Jones

*Chapter 4*

# Up for the Cup

**To win the Championship is a show of consistency and staying-power, but the Cup is the real test: a triumph of nerve, steel and character that stretches the emotions beyond all rational bounds**

How often have we heard managers and players refer to a crucial League game as their "Cup Final"? It is the ultimate test, the moment of truth, when the gauntlet has been thrown down and your life is on the line. Yes, to win a cup might well be a short sprint in terms of a season; but it can stimulate a lifetime of passion, emotion and memories, so why should it be devalued in terms of the League?

## Before the Premiership

In the latter decades of the nineteenth century, when the Association game was in its infancy and a bit beyond, the Cup – the Football Association Challenge Cup, that is – was held in high esteem as the Blue Riband event of the game.

Alas, Leeds found it a trophy beyond reach until 1972. Indeed, United fans must have resigned themselves to failure in the great knock-out tournament, for they had to wait until the campaign of 1949–50 before they could celebrate more than two wins in a row. Carlisle United, Bolton (in a replay) and Cardiff City were dismissed to earn United a sixth-round tilt at Arsenal.

United's dismal showing in the competition was not enhanced by 10 successive defeats between 1952 and 1962. It was not until the Revie revolution that the club finally made its mark.

In 1965 United reached Wembley for the first time in the club's history. Their opponents were Liverpool and it was a desperately close thing. In the end, however, it was the Merseysiders who came out on top, 2–1 after extra time. Both teams, recently returned to the first division, were unused to the big Cup Final atmosphere and tension. The game could hardly have been described as a classic match – it was more like a game of chess, a battle of wits and tactics, with both sides cancelling each other out. Liverpool who took the lead through Roger Hunt early in the first period of extra time. A brilliant run and shot from Billy Bremner brought a rallyingequalizer eight minutes later, but Ian St. John snatched the winner nine minutes from the final whistle.

**FA CUP FINAL**

**1 May 1965**
Wembley Stadium

**Leeds United 1**
(Bremner)
**Liverpool 2**
(Hunt, St. John)
*(after extra time)*

HT 0–0. 90 min 0–0
Att: 100,000

**Team:**
Sprake, Reaney, Bell, Bremner, Charlton, Hunter, Giles, Storrie, Peacock, Collins, Johanneson

## League Cup glory

Three years later, however, there was Wembley glory in the Football League Cup. Dismissed by many clubs as an unnecessary intrusion in its early years, the League Cup suddenly gained big-time status in 1967 when the final was played at Wembley instead of over two legs.

Leeds' record in the competition up until then had been extremely modest. Beaten 7–0 at West Ham the year before, when they equalled their best run to reach the fourth round, they finally found form in 1967–68, despatching Luton, Bury, Sunderland and Stoke before overcoming Derby County in a two-legged semi-final (1–0 at the Baseball Ground and 3–2 at Elland Road).

**LEAGUE CUP FINAL**

**2 March 19 1968**
Wembley Stadium

**Leeds United 1**
(Cooper)
**Arsenal 0**

HT 1–0. Att: 100,000

**Team:**
Sprake, Reaney, Cooper, Bremner, Charlton, Hunter, Greenhoff, Lorimer, Madeley, Giles, E Gray (Belfitt)

The final was no great spectacle: tactical manoeuvres overcame inspiration and physical combat eclipsed artistry. The cup was won 18 minutes in when Arsenal's defence failed to clear a Leeds corner properly. 'Keeper Jim Furnell flapped at the ball and fullback Terry Cooper thumped a crisp volley into the net through a forest of bodies. Leeds were bringing home their first major trophy.

## Replay misery

The FA Cup continued to prove an elusive prize with a second final defeat, this time at the hands of Chelsea and after extra time in a replay. United had made a good start in terrible conditions – the game was nicknamed "the Sandcastle Final" after the amount of sand laid on the pitch to mop up the heavy rain that had fallen in the preceding weeks.

Leeds were the better team at Wembley, and their inability to hold first-half leads in both matches cost them dear. Jack Charlton had opened the scoring with a first-half header that bounced between Eddie McCreadie and Ron Harris on the line for Chelsea, but a speculative long-range shot from Peter Houseman, just before the break, levelled matters again.

Eddie Gray gave David Webb a terrible time, and teased and tormented the full-back to such an extent that Chelsea changed their positions in the replay. But when Mick Jones headed Leeds back in front near the end, extra time, let alone a replay, seemed unnecessary. However, Ian Hutchinson scored a 86th-minute equalizer to force the extra strength-sapping 30 minutes of play.

The replay was held at Old Trafford and Jones again put Leeds ahead. Leeds dominated the game but a goal from Peter Osgood in the second half and a bundled header in the last minute of extra time from David Webb, who may have fouled Harvey in the process, were enough to give the Cup to Chelsea.

**Jack Charlton (far right) celebrates after scoring from a corner kick in the FA Cup Final against Chelsea**

**FA CUP FINAL**

**11 April 1970**
Wembley Stadium

**Leeds United 2**
(Charlton, Jones),
**Chelsea 2**
(Houseman, Hutchinson)
*(after extra time)*

HT: 1–1. 90 min: 2–2
Att: 100,000

**Team:**
Sprake, Madeley, Cooper, Bremner, Charlton, Hunter, Lorimer, Clarke, Jones, Giles, E Gray

**FA CUP FINAL REPLAY**

**29 April 1970**
Old Trafford, Manchester

**Leeds United 1**
(Jones),
**Chelsea 2**
(Osgood, Webb)
*(after extra time)*

HT: 1–0. 90 min: 1–1.
Att 56,000

**Team:**
Harvey, Madeley, Cooper, Bremner, Charlton, Hunter, Lorimer, Clarke, Jones, Giles, E Gray

## FA Cup-winners at last

It was third time lucky for Leeds in the FA Cup Final of 1972 against the Cup-holders, Arsenal. The legendary double was still a distinct possibility, with the Cup Final coming just two days before the final League match against Wolves. A win at Wembley and a draw at Molineux would do the job nicely.

Arsenal had not made a good defence of their League crown so the Cup was the last chance of salvaging something from the season. The challenges fairly flew in, Peter Lorimer being on the receiving end from Bob McNab a few times. But he was not cowed into submission, and in the second half United took over. Mick Jones received a pass from Lorimer, crossed from the bye-line and watched as Allan Clarke threw himself into a 12-yard header that was far too good for Geoff Barnett.

**FA CUP FINAL**

**6 May 1972**
Wembley Stadium

**Leeds United 1**
(Clarke)
**Arsenal 0**

HT: 0–0. Att 100,000

**Team:**
Harvey, Reaney, Madeley, Bremner, Charlton, Hunter, Lorimer, Clarke, Jones, Giles, E Gray

Jones suffered a serious shoulder injury just before the end, but it could not put a damper on the celebrations following the final whistle. Maybe it was the celebrations or just the exhaustion, but Wolves escaped with a 2–1 victory to deny Leeds the double.

## Sunderland shock Leeds

Leeds had launched cup attacks on all fronts, reaching the European Cup-Winners' Cup Final as well as returning to Wembley in the FA Cup. Their opponents were the people's favourites, second-division Sunderland, but Leeds could not afford to succumb to sentimentality.

As it was, all the breaks went Sunderland's way. After 32 minutes Ian Porterfield swung his "wrong" leg at the ball and his volley flew into the net. The second half saw Leeds lay siege to the Sunderland goal, but it led a charmed life. Trevor Cherry had a goal disallowed and 'keeper Jim Montgomery produced one of the greatest double-saves in FA Cup history to deny first Cherry's header, then Lorimer's shot at an almost-unguarded goal.

Amazingly, after four finals in eight seasons, Leeds have yet to return to the FA Cup Final.

**FA CUP FINAL**

**6 May 1972**
Wembley Stadium

**Leeds United 0**
**Sunderland 1**
(Porterfield)

HT: 0–1. Att 100,000

**Team:**
Harvey, Reaney, Cherry, Bremner, Madeley, Hunter, Lorimer, Clarke, Jones, Giles, E Gray (Yorath)

# *Into the Premiership, 1992–93*

The Coca-Cola (League) Cup brought its regular share of banana-skins. The first match with Scunthorpe United took five weeks to complete, with European and international commitments taking priority. Nonetheless, the hard part was done in the first leg at Elland Road when Carl Shutt, Gary Speed, Lee Chapman and Gordon Strachan were on target in a 4–1 first-leg win. The return at Glanford Park ended 2–2, Rod Wallace and Chapman scoring, but a week after losing in the European Cup to Glasgow Rangers Watford repeated the dose at Vicarage Road, Gary McAllister scoring in a 2–1 reverse.

FA Cup success has been just as elusive. Charlton Athletic created great anxiety after forcing a 1–1 draw at Elland Road. Speed, the scorer, also opened the account in the replay, and McAllister wrapped up a 3–1 victory after Garland's own goal had given United the edge.

**Legs Eleven: Gary Speed launches himself into the pack to score the equalizer at Charlton in the FA Cup third round match at Elland Road on 2 January 1993**

It was back to London in round four and a tough assignment at Highbury. Speed was again on target while Arsenal old-boy Chapman claimed his 13th goal of the season to force a very encouraging 2–2 draw. The fans might have believed the hard part had been completed, but not the players; and though Shutt and McAllister carved their names on to the scoresheet, John Lukic was beaten three times by his former colleagues, the winner coming in extra time.

# *1993–94*

The following year brought even less cup success. The Coca-Cola Cup paired Leeds with Sunderland and the Rokerites earned a passage into the next round with a pair of 2–1 victories. Gary Speed was on target in the first game and Phil Whelan netted his first senior goal for Leeds in the second leg.

In the FA Cup, United were handed a seemingly comfortable draw in the opening tie, a home game against Crewe Alexandra. Young Jamie Forrester was United's secret weapon. Jamie blasted Crewe out of the Cup with a two-goal salvo. Brian Deane conjured up his first goal for seven matches to earn the lead,

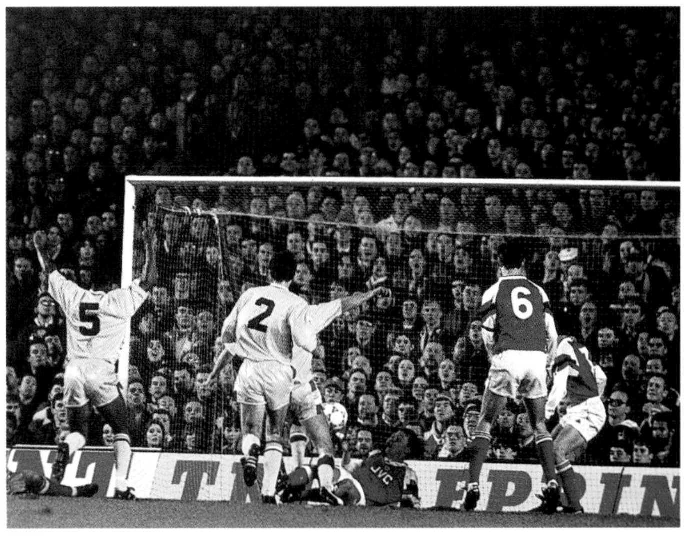

**Lee Chapman (hidden) floors Arsenal with the second goal in the 2–2 draw at Highbury**

**Jamie Forrester scores against Crewe: he was United's secret weapon**

and though it was a bit tense when Stuart Naylor equalized, up stepped Forrester in the 58th and 83rd minutes to round off a super show.

In the fourth round Leeds' first-half show at the cramped Manor Ground was hardly bubbly. Oxford United, without a win in 11 first-division games and acutely haunted by fears of relegation, passed the ball with far more accuracy and authority, on a heavy pitch lubricated by drizzle, than did the stars from Elland Road, and there could really be no complaints when they forged into a two-goal lead.

Joey Beauchamp was the instigator. From the right wing he found Jim Magilton who swept the ball to the unmarked Dyer, and he had no trouble shooting under Beeney's outstretched right hand. Hesitancy in defence cost Leeds a second goal following a half-cleared corner. The ball was prodded back for Mike Lewis to head over watching markers and Matt Elliott shot in off a post. It was a memorable goal for the big centre-half, not least because he has supported Leeds all his life.

Gary Speed had caused Oxford a few problems, and minutes later he reduced the advantage. A cross was headed down and Speed, with hardly any back-lift, lashed his shot high into the net. Beeney then did well to thwart Dave Cusack as Leeds came into their own. During the final 30 minutes Oxford struggled as United's pace, strength and stamina repeatedly threatened to sweep them away. Four minutes after coming on as a substitute, David Wetherall rose above the pack to thump a glorious header beyond Phil Whitehead. United might have won it but for Whitehead's defiance, the best of a clutch of fine saves denying David White who, on the turn, crashed a glorious shot goalwards.

The fans had to endure another of those embarrassing nights in the replay at Elland Road, United spluttering to a 3–2 extra-time defeat despite having seemingly plucked salvation from the jaws of disaster thanks to goals from Gordon Strachan and David White. It was an authentic footballing fairy-tale for Oxford United; the ultimate nightmare for Leeds.

# 1994–95

Yet again, United were toppled at the first hurdle in the Coca-Cola Cup, the 1–0 aggregate defeat by Mansfield Town of the third division providing even more ammunition for those disgruntled followers who were beginning to point the finger Howard Wilkinson's way.

When the FA Cup draw turned up a third-round away trip to Third Division Walsall, the pessimists were loud with prophecies of doom. Such negativity hardly helped the situation, and it was understandable that there should be signs of uncertainty in the Leeds camp. It was a close call too, United being rescued from ignominy only by an 87th-minute equalizer from defender David Wetherall.

There was to be no giant-killing act this time, however. At Elland Road, Phil Masinga soothed the frayed nerve-endings with an extra-special hat-trick. It was a tension-packed thriller as Leeds were twice hauled back by the Saddlers and forced into extra time. Brian Deane had scored an eighth-minute opener that was cancelled out by a Martyn O'Connor penalty, and after David Wetherall had headed in McAllister's cross Kevin Wilson popped in a second equalizer. Then up stepped substitute Masinga to strike three glorious goals and leave Walsall shattered 5–2.

By half-time in the fourth-round home tie against Oldham Athletic, goals by David White and Carlton Palmer had established a comfortable lead; but any thoughts of an easy passage were quickly dismissed in an explosive opening to the second period during which, in a pulsating four-minute spell, three goals were scored.

First Gunnar Halle, the Norwegian international who two years later would wear the white shirt of Leeds, raced on to Brennan's cross and thrashed the ball past John Lukic, who had been dragged out of position. Within a minute, Leeds made it 3–1. David White careered down the wing and planted a cross on to Phil Masinga's head and the South African delivered the perfect finish.

Almost immediately, however, Brennan's in-swinging corner was nodded straight past the surprised John Lukic by Palmer for an own goal. 3–2, and the easy ride was now a bumpy road – though, defensively, United were again looking solid. Minutes from time Nicky Banger would have squared the tie but for a masterful save from Lukic, who had rushed out to block the Oldham striker's 12-yard shot.

The fifth-round draw was hardly kind – a trip to Manchester United. Yet midfield hero Carlton Palmer was far from daunted by the prospect, after helping Leeds United reach the last 16 for the first time in eight years. "We've all got a feeling about the FA Cup this season", he quipped, "David Wetherall's equalizer at Walsall was the turning point in our fortunes."

Palmer explained: "The boss kept telling us things would change if we maintained our form – and that's what happened. I believe we are well-equipped to take on anybody. We can knock the ball about with the best when we get the chance, and if opponents try to stop us playing, we've got the strength to play a power game."

On the face of it, this team certainly appeared to have the resources to go all the way: a solid defence that had maintained five clean sheets in its last seven Premiership games and an attack in which Phil Masinga and Brian Deane were gelling well together, while the powerhouse Tony Yeboah was breathing down their necks from the substitutes' bench.

At Old Trafford things were not on Leeds' side. An early goal down and all at sea in the opening phase, their second-half domination was not rewarded on the scoresheet. Yeboah, again brought off the bench, scored the only reply to the Reds' three goals.

# 1995–96

It's strange how League and Cup form can be so out of tune. In the campaign of 1995–96, United fell from grace in the FA Carling Premiership by finishing 13th, yet enjoyed their best runs ever, as a Premiership club, in both the Coca-Cola and FA Cups. The former provided the highlights of what proved to be a hostile season. It started in Nottingham in mid-September and ended at Wembley five months later.

The twin towers seemed an impossible dream when, at Elland Road on 19 September 1995, Notts County played out a goalless draw. The only saving grace on a miserable night was that County did not snatch a vital away goal. Even so, given their recent record against the minnows, there was much anxiety surrounding the second leg, with County fancying themselves to slay the Yorkshire giant once again.

So, too, it might have been, but for a last-gasp goal by Gary Speed. United had teetered on the brink against 10-man County whose centre-back Gary

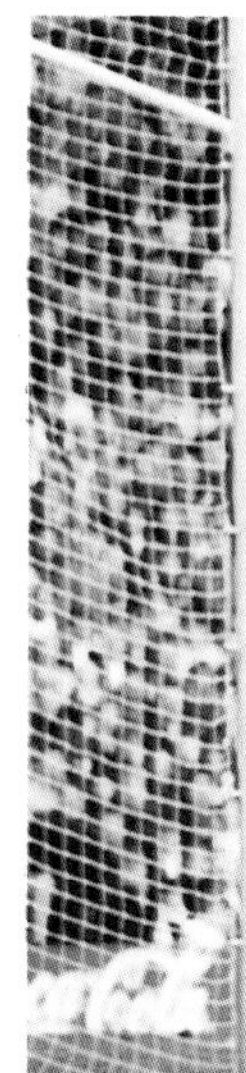

**Brian Deane's header gives Birmingham City the blues**

Strodder had been sent off for two bookable offences. It was well into injury time when Speed beat goalkeeper Darren Ward from 25 yards.

Gary McAllister, who had given United a 20th-minute lead, had to retire at the break through injury. Then Devon White equalized from a penalty after being held down by David Wetherall, and the same man shot County into a 75th-minute lead. The best goal of the night, a confident and decisive half-volley from Andy Couzens, brought United back on par.

Speed was again the hero in a very close contest in round three at Derby County. It could have gone either way, with defences on top. Then in ghosted Gary to flick home the winner with a back-post header.

Tomas Brolin made his much-awaited debut in the fourth-round tie against Blackburn Rovers, and did not disappoint. Leeds were totally on top for 70 minutes and sitting on a cushion of two goals, courtesy of Tony Yeboah and Brian Deane, when Rovers clawed one back. Inspired by Alan Shearer, Rovers mounted a tremendous fightback and it was only the athleticism and razor-sharp reflexes of John Lukic which kept them at bay. One save in particular, from a Colin Hendry special, was world-class.

David Wetherall admits that when they realized it was Reading in the fifth round, dressing-room chat began to turn to Wembley. Arsenal, Newcastle United, and Aston Villa were still in the competition, so to get a first-division club at home, and an unfashionable and struggling one at that, was a great incentive.

In the end it turned out to be another major battle, Reading more than matching United in endeavour. I suppose you could say this was the Biscuitmen's proverbial "cup final" and the 2–1 scoreline is a fair reflection of the closeness of it all. Still, a side-footer from Phil Masinga and a header from Speed overturned Reading's opening strike from Jimmy Quinn.

When United missed Arsenal and Aston Villa in the semi-final draw and were paired with Birmingham City, the feeling was that Leeds were almost at Wembley. However, there had to be no counting of chickens before they hatched, and though the lads made a confident start at St Andrew's, creating three glorious chances, all of them were spurned. Even goal-ace Tony Yeboah failed from six yards. The doubts crept in when, despite exploiting the gulf in class to the full and dominating the Blues, Leeds found themselves a goal down as Kevin Francis lashed in a super shot that no 'keeper on earth would have been able to prevent.

Manager Wilkinson had to call on all his experience to lift his side at the break, but Birmingham City were brimming with confidence and the play was much more even. Tony Yeboah struck in the 54th minute – no more than Leeds deserved – but the winner proved elusive until the 72nd minute. A dangerous ball was bent into the Birmingham box and former Leeds defender Chris Whyte, conscious of Yeboah's presence, tried to intercept but turned the ball into his own net.

So United went into the second leg at Elland Road ahead, and with the added advantage of two away goals. Leeds had one foot in Wembley. Would Wilkinson shut up shop, or would he go for the jugular? Howard could have fallen back on caution, but instead was bold and thrillingly positive, using Phil Masinga instead of the more defensive Mark Ford.

It kept Birmingham on the back foot, and once Masinga scored in the 48th minute the nerves were eased and United romped to a colourful 3–0 victory. It could all have been so different, however, for five minutes earlier Richardson had looked set to make it 2–2 on aggregate as he crashed in a shot, Lukic making a sensational block. Then came the moment of truth for Birmingham. Yeboah let fly, the ball ricocheted into the danger zone where it was met by McAllister whose shot from 11 yards was parried by Dutch goalkeeper Bart Griemink. Alas for him, it was to no avail, for Masinga pounced to slide in the rebound.

Elland Road was brought to its feet by the second

**Brian Deane is at full stretch to beat Ugo Ehiogu in the 1996 Coca-Cola Cup Final clash with Aston Villa, which ended in defeat for United by three goals to nil**

goal. Kelly hit a long free kick into the Birmingham area and Deane got two headers in before Yeboah, with his back to goal, twisted instinctively and was horizontally airborne as he struck a fantastic volley – an unstoppable shot from 10 yards into the net. The whole crowd stood to applaud; privileged to have seen, and enjoyed, such dynamic athleticism.

Suddenly, though, there was drama at the other end. Kelly tripped John Sheridan and the referee was pointing to the spot. A goal now might rattle United, confidence often being such a brittle commodity. Steve Claridge, socks sagging, shirt drooping over his shorts, took the responsibility. You could cut the tension with a knife as he ran at the ball and thumped it hard towards the target. Lukic dived but was nowhere near the ball as it thudded against a post.

They knew then that Wembley was a reality; and when McAllister found Deane at the far post with a searching cross, the striker did what comes naturally to him – stuck it in the net! 3–0 to Leeds, Birmingham beaten 5–1 on aggregate.

## Coca-Cola Cup Final

A tremendous triumph for Howard Wilkinson brought to an end United's 23-year quest for the Wembley grail. Now he hoped to enjoy one of his proudest moments in football as he led United out alongside Aston Villa manager Brian Little.

The build-up to the big day had not gone entirely smoothly. Since overcoming Birmingham City, United had won just one of their four Premiership fixtures and their overall haul of just seven goals in 10 League matches was costing them dearly. Wilko had axed his record signing, Brolin,

**COCA-COLA CUP FINAL**

**11 April 1996**
Wembley Stadium

**Leeds United 0,**
**Aston Villa 3**
(Milosevic, Taylor, Yorke)

HT: 0–1. Att: 77,065

**Team:**
Lukic, Kelly, Wetherall, Radebe (Brolin), Palmer, Pemberton, McAllister, Speed, Ford (Deane), Gray, Yeboah

following a 5–0 hammering at Liverpool and the Swede was far from pleased.

The defensive flaws that had seen 15 goals rip into their net in seven Premiership games were exploited again in the 20th minute at Wembley. Villa's Savo Milosevic picked up the ball and drifted slowly into Leeds territory. He wasn't challenged as United backed off; a little push to the left took him wide of two opponents, and the shot he unleashed from 28 yards ripped into the top left corner.

In truth, Leeds didn't turn up for the party. Villa extended their lead in the 55th minute when Wetherall, desperate to clear, got in the way of Lukic. The ball fell to Ian Taylor who left Carlton Palmer standing to hit a crisp cross shot into the net. Dwight Yorke made it 3–0 in the final minute.

At the post-match press conference Howard Wilkinson admitted: "It is very difficult to sort my thoughts out. Villa were sharper than us, passed better than us and in most areas were better than us." The drained chief went on: "It didn't pass very quickly for me today. I didn't enjoy one bit of it. You always have to try and look for some good points and Andy Gray was our man of the match – it's only his fifth start.

"It doesn't matter what system you play; it depends on your players and the way that they play on the day."

## Bad week all round

People have short memories in this game, but Leeds fans had suffered a double blow in four days, losing at Wembley and previously experiencing the ignominy of a 3–0 defeat at Anfield in an FA Cup sixth-round replay. It was the club's best run in this competition since reaching the semi-final in 1987, when eventual winners Coventry City triumphed 3–2 in extra time.

United had defeated Derby County 4–2 in a dramatic third-round tie played out on a pitch that resembled a cabbage patch after three months' solid rain. With Leeds sliding into the bottom half of the Premiership a victory was essential, but the League position was reflected in Wilkinson's cautious approach. Brolin was left out, Palmer played sweeper in a five-man defence with McAllister, Speed and Ford were in midfield and Deane and Yeboah up-front.

It looked fine in theory but proved to be dreadful in practice, after the Rams took a two-goal lead. It was the 57th minute before Speed replied with a left-foot shot. A minute later Deane converted Dorigo's cross and the tide had turned. Even so, the odds were on a replay until McAllister and Yeboah sensationally scored in stoppage time.

"All our season summed up in 90 minutes", reflected Wilkinson. "Enough to drive a manager potty. We went out at half-time after preaching the gospel of patience and we showed the exact opposite. We got the result, and that's all that will show in *Rothmans* in 15 or 18 years."

A goal in 58 seconds sank Bolton at Burnden Park. Yeboah helped on Dorigo's long throw and, as defender Alan Stubbs and goalkeeper Keith Branagan hesitated, Rod Wallace nipped in for a simple finish at the far post. United had to survive a replay fright at first-division Port Vale after a 0–0 draw at home, with Gary McAllister's two second-half goals – a rare header and a typically lethal free kick – saving their blushes.

The 88th-minute winner was a memorable moment. McAllister's body language, after Palmer had earned a free kick 25 yards out, was emphatic. His boot made perfect contact with the ball; Paul Musselwhite's despairing dive added to the occasion as the ball scorched into the net.

There were no such memories of the sixth-round encounter with Liverpool. "Bore War!" was how one paper summed up the goalless draw at Elland Road. The return at Anfield was a better game, but it was Liverpool who ran out 3–0 winners.

# *1996–97*

Those familiar cup demons returned to trouble Leeds early in the season, when Darlington twice came from behind to draw 2–2 at Elland Road in the second

**Facing his old club, Crystal Palace, Nigel Martyn stops Bruce Dyer's penalty with a blinding save**

round of the Coca-Cola Cup. Ian Rush needed one goal to equal Geoff Hurst's League Cup record, but it was Rod Wallace who grabbed both goals and Wallace and Ian Harte scored in the 2–0 second-leg victory at the Feethams.

Round three produced a replay of the previous season's final. Alas for Leeds, the result was repeated too and Rush again failed to find the target. Although Lee Sharpe shot United ahead after 69 minutes, Ian Taylor equalized almost immediately and Dwight Yorke secured the Midlanders' ticket to round four from the penalty spot 13 minutes from time.

An explosive 2–2 draw at Crystal Palace marked United's FA Cup debut under George Graham. Brian Deane scored in only the second minute, Palace surged back as Bruce Dyer scored from the spot. An own goal by Lief Andersen put Leeds ahead again – and there had been just eight minutes played. Carl Veart made it 2–2 and, with two minutes to go, Palace were awarded a second penalty, Lucas Radebe being adjudged to have tripped Dyer. The Palace forward took on Nigel Martyn again but this time the former Palace 'keeper dived to his right to make a superb save. A stunning Rod Wallace replay goal was enough to earn a fourth-round visit to Highbury.

Three days earlier, United had battled out a 0–0 draw at Arsenal in the Premiership and George Graham returned to haunt his old club again: not a tie for the faint-hearted. Kelly man-marked Paul Merson and Gunnar Halle shadowed Ian Wright out of the picture, leaving the Gunners firing blanks after Rod Wallace's 11th-minute winner. Accelerating on to a long ball, he managed to squeeze his shot past David Seaman, and Martin Keown's desperate lunge diverted the ball on to a post. It rebounded to Wallace, who gleefully whacked it high into the roof of the Arsenal net.

A fifth-round tie at Portsmouth saw United made second favourites for the Cup. It was misplaced confidence, however, as the first-division side romped through 3–2: and it would have been more but for another Nigel Martyn penalty save. Alan McLoughlin put the first-division team ahead after seven minutes: a lead which lasted exactly 45 minutes, before Lee Bowyer equalized. Scandinavian striker Mathias Svensson put Portsmouth ahead again and Lee Bradbury made it safe with four minutes left. Bowyer's injury-time second goal was scant consolation.

**A delighted Rod Wallace delivers the KO to Arsenal in United's 1–0 FA Cup fourth round victory**

# The Premiership Stars

*Chapter 5*

**A wealth of talent has worn the famous white shirt in United's five seasons in the FA Premiership. Here we look at some of the stars who have served the club so well.**

All statistics correct to the start of 1997–98 season

## *David* Batty

Leeds-born and bred, David first linked up with the club as an associated schoolboy in November 1983. Small in stature, big of heart, he was compared in his apprenticeship years to the great Billy Bremner, who incidentally launched his career with Leeds, and like the great man David has never let his lack of inches deflect him from his objective, the tenacious side of his personality always being to the fore.

Indeed, at one stage the tiger in his tackle ran riot and his awful disciplinary record became a millstone around his neck. For in his first two seasons in League football David amassed 82 disciplinary points – and this despite only being sent off once in a reserve match!

It was Howard Wilkinson who set him straight and persuaded him to polish up his act: good advice and well taken, for David established himself not only as a key figure in the Leeds United engine room but also as a ball-winning midfielder for England.

**A wing-half in the Bremner mould, David Batty's grit and determination made him a fans' favourite**

David recalls: "When I was a kid on the staff I once overheard Mr Bremner, who was the manager, telling one of the coaches that I was his type of player. I think he saw something of himself in me; though I never saw him play, I know enough about him to be honoured by any comparisons.

"He moved me from right-back into midfield and gave me my League debut." That was a home game against Swindon Town on 21 November 1987.

Towards the end of the 1988–89 season manager Wilkinson dropped Batty, whose response was to hand in a shock transfer request.

It was not granted, and that summer David hit the headlines for all the best reasons when voted the "Most Elegant Player" while performing for the England Under-21 side in the Toulon international tournament.

Already capped at youth level, David was now to be promoted to the England "B" squad and play a key role in United's Second Division championship success, collecting the Barclay's Young Eagle of the Month award for October *en route.*

Towards the end of his first season in Division One Batty made his full England debut, against the USSR at Wembley on 21 May 1991, and made two appearances in the European Championship squad in Sweden, one in the troublesome right-back position. Surprisingly, David was left out of Terry Venables' Euro '96 squad, but is now firmly established in Glenn Hoddle's plans.

David took a leading role in United's League Championship success – their first since 1974 – and took over the captaincy while Gary McAllister was on the sick list. It seemed he was established at Elland Road for life. But nothing is for ever in this game; and in 1994, after more than 200 appearances for Leeds, Batty joined Blackburn Rovers for £2.75 million, picking up a second Championship medal and the Player of the Year title in his first season at Ewood Park. In March 1997 Newcastle swooped with a cheque for £3.5 million and now David is looking to win three championships with three different clubs.

**David BATTY**

**Born:**
2 December 1968, in Leeds
**Position:**
Midfield
**Height/Weight:**
5ft 6in/10st 5lb
**Leeds Career:**
1985–1993
**Leeds debut:**
vs. Swindon Town (W 4–1) Div.2 (21.11.87)

# *Mervyn* Day

**Mervyn DAY**

**Born:**
25 June 1955, in Chelmsford, Essex.
**Position:**
Goalkeeper
**Height/Weight:**
6ft 2in/15st 1lb
**Leeds Career:**
1985–1993
**Leeds debut:**
vs. Oldham Athletic (1–1) Div.2 (2.2.85)

Former England Youth international Mervyn Day joined West Ham United as an apprentice in 1971. Such was the impact he made on breaking into the senior side as a teenager that normally-reserved manager Ron Greenwood declared him "the England goalkeeper for the next ten years." Alas, the spectacular youngster never quite lived up to Ron's great expectations, collecting just five Under-23 caps.

Making his League debut on a rain-lashed night in August 1973 in a 3–3 draw with Ipswich, Mervyn went on to clock up almost 250 League and Cup appearances for the Hammers in five-and-a-half years. The highlight came in 1975 with an FA Cup-winners' medal for beating Fulham 2–0 and the PFA's Young Footballer of the Year award. There was more metalwork the following year: an ECWC runners'-up medal after West Ham went down to Anderlecht.

In July 1979 Day moved to Leyton Orient in a £100,000 deal, where he performed with distinction in another 200 games, but he got his biggest boost to date in August 1983 when Aston Villa signed him as cover for Spink for £15,000. Such was his form that he won the first-team jersey.

His career took another upward turn in February 1985 as Eddie Gray invested £30,000 to take him to Leeds, where Mervyn enjoyed eight highly successful years. The backbone of United's second-division championship side in 1989–90, he notched up his 600th League appearance *en route* to the title. A model of consistency, Day's spot-

**Mervyn Day kept goal for Leeds with distinction in his eight year career at the club**

less record between the posts led one team-mate to joke: "He has had so many clean sheets you would think he owned a laundry."

Mervyn lost his place to Lukic and made just two Premiership appearances in 1992–93, finishing his Leeds career as a coach before moving to Carlisle United in the same capacity in 1993. In January 1996 he moved along the bench to become manager, a role he has performed to great effect. Not that Leeds will have a chance to forget the Day family name: Mervyn's son Richard, a midfielder, signed associated schoolboy forms with United in April 1994.

## *Brian* **Deane**

Brian Deane took a while to settle in at Elland Road following his much-publicised £2.7 million transfer from Sheffield United in July 1993, and at first was unable to reproduce the fire-power he demonstrated so spectacularly with the Blades – 83 goals in 197 League appearances.

Eventually, however, he won the crowd over, proving there was far more to his game than just drifting around as a target man. At six feet three and 12 stone 8lbs he is speedy, powerful and equally skilful with either foot – his elder brother Tony made him practice with both feet from the age of six. Though physically suited to the traditional centre-forward's role, Deane has operated successfully in a wider position. At the close of his second season at Elland Road, during which he scored 10 goals – 9 in the Premiership – he received the accolade of Player of the Year.

**Brian DEANE**

**Born:**
7 February 1968, in Leeds.
**Position:**
Striker
**Height/Weight:**
6ft 3in/12st 1lb
**Leeds Career:**
1993–1997
**Leeds debut:**
vs. Manchester City (1–1) Prem (14.8.93)

Ironically, Leeds could quite easily have picked up this big-money signing for nothing. A local lad, the son of an engineering worker, he was brought up in the city's Chapeltown district. He played in the Leeds City Boys team which reached the semi-finals of the 1980 English Schools Trophy (David Batty was in the same squad), and signed associated schoolboy forms

**Brian Deane, seen here against West Ham, contributed greatly to the team in his five year stint**

with United – but wrote to Doncaster Rovers for a trial instead when Leeds did not offer him a YTS place.

After his apprenticeship with Rovers, Brian first emerged on to the League scene in a home game with Swansea City (0–0) in February 1986. He spent two years at Belle Vue, scoring 10 goals in 66 League outings; enough to persuade Dave Bassett to gamble £30,000 of Sheffield United's money on his transfer.

It proved money well spent, for Deane built up a phenomenal striking partnership with Tony Agana which shot Sheffield United from the third to the first division in two years. Brian's legacy to the Blades was 83 goals in 197 League matches, not to mention another 22 goals in the two major cup competitions.

He was top scorer in four successive seasons and earned himself a place in the history books as scorer of the first goal in the Premiership, just four minutes into a game against Manchester United on the opening day of the 1992–93 campaign.

Picked for England's summer tour in 1991, Brian won two full caps against New Zealand and picked up a third when he came on as a substitute in the 1–0 defeat by Spain in Santander in September 1992. Other honours include three England "B" appearances.

Though injury restricted his progress at Leeds, the return to his home town proved a wonderful career move for the Yorkshireman, but still not at ease he returned to Bramall Lane in the summer of 1997.

# *Tony* **Dorigo**

**Tony DORIGO**

**Born:**
31 December 1965, in Melbourne, Australia
**Position:**
Full-back
**Height/Weight:**
5ft 1in/10st 10lb
**Leeds Career:**
1991–
**Leeds debut:**
vs. Nottingham Forest (W 1–0) Div.1 (20.8.91)

A full England international with 14 caps, Dorigo hails from Melbourne in Australia. Such was his passion for football that he financed his own passage to England in pursuit of his ambition to become a professional. The son of an Italian immigrant, Tony had played the game from the age of six and by 15 was playing in the same side as his father in senior men's football.

"That brought home to me that there wasn't a lot of future in Australian football for me," says Tony. "If I could command a regular place in the men's senior

**Tony Dorigo, a classic footballing left-back – probably the best since Terry Cooper**

league at 15 then the standard was not too high. So I decided to leave."

His instinct was to head for Italy, but the language barrier deterred him from that course and instead he wrote to a dozen first-division clubs in the Football League requesting a trial.

Aston Villa were the only club to respond to his pleas and were so impressed that they signed him straight away, in 1983. Introduced to League football at Ipswich, on 12 May 1984, Tony quickly proved himself a stylish performer, comfortable on the ball and accurate in his passing. When Villa were relegated in 1987 Tony was anxious to maintain a presence in the top flight and joined Chelsea for £475,000.

His full international entry came in a clash with Yugoslavia in 1989, and he was picked for Graham Taylor's squad in the European Championship Finals in Sweden in 1992, having previously been honoured at Under-21 (11 caps) and "B" (seven appearances) levels. In the summer of 1991 Howard Wilkinson paid £1.3 million for Tony's services.

A sweet striker of the ball – his was the only goal when Chelsea beat Middlesbrough in the ZDS Cup Final at Wembley in 1990, and he scored again at Wembley when Leeds beat Liverpool 4–3 in the Charity Shield in 1992 – Dorigo is a dead-ball kick specialist. Considered the best Leeds left-back since Terry Cooper, he was voted Player of the Year in the 1991–92 championship season but knee, hamstring, and ankle injuries have limited his appearances.

# *Chris* **Fairclough**

Chris has played more than 300 League games in a career which started at Nottingham Forest in 1978. Parkhead Academicals was his first club, and he made his League entry at Anfield in September 1982.

Hailed by Brian Clough as one of the greatest young players in the country, Fairclough's promise was reflected by seven England Under-21 caps; but after missing most of the 1985–86 season through injury he couldn't win his place back again and transferred to Tottenham Hotspur in 1987 for £387,000.

However, he never really settled at White Hart Lane, and two years later was contributing significantly to United's second-division championship success following a £500,000 move after a loan spell. He won further glory in an outstanding 1991–92 campaign, collecting a League championship medal.

For a while he was used at full-back, and moved again to fill in as a defensive midfielder when Batty left the side, but is more at home in the centre of defence. In July 1995 Chris terminated his association with the club when he joined Bolton Wanderers for £1 million.

**Chris FAIRCLOUGH**

**Born:**
12 April 1964, in Nottingham
**Position:**
Central defender
**Height/Weight:**
5ft 11in/11st 2lb
**Leeds Career:**
1989–1995
**Leeds debut:**
vs. Portsmouth (W 1–0) Div.2 (25.3.89)

**Chris Fairclough, a strong defender who is comfortable on the ball**

# *Richard* **Jobson**

**Richard JOBSON**

**Born:**
9 May 1963, in Hull
**Position:**
Central defender
**Height/Weight:**
6ft 1in/13st 5lb
**Leeds Career:**
1995–1997
**Leeds debut:**
vs Chelsea (W1–0) Prem (18.11.95)

The fact that it did not work out for Richard at United is a shame, because at one stage during his career with Oldham Athletic he looked an England certainty. Big, strong, with good balance and a positive touch, he was the archetypal footballing centre-half. Howard Wilkinson paid £1 million for him in October 1995 after the apparent collapse of his transfer that summer, and 14 months after he had first tried to get him to Leeds – an ankle injury had stood in the way on that occasion.

But his luck was still out. After 13 games a serious knee injury ruled Richard out for the rest of the season. Though he was determined to prove his worth in 1996–97 things refused to come together, and he left to continue his career with Spurs.

Richard began his career playing non-League football with Burton Albion while studying at Nottingham University for a civil engineering degree, but cut short his studies to sign for Watford when they came in with a £22,000 offer in November 1982. He was at the hub of the Watford side that finished runners-up to Liverpool in Division One and it was a surprise when he moved to Hull for £40,000 in

**Richard Jobson launches a Leeds attack during their 2–1 loss to Coventry City in September 1996**

February 1985.

He played more than 220 League games for his home-town club, including a promotion to Division Two, before being recruited by Oldham Athletic for £460,000. There he won a second-division championship medal in 1991 and starred in their Cup giant-killing acts. Graham Taylor, his old manager at Watford, included Jobson in his England squad for the European Championship qualifying match with Norway, and though he never won a full cap Richard was given two games with the "B" team.

# *Gary* **Kelly**

**Gary KELLY**

**Born:**
9 July 1974, in Drogheda, Ireland
**Position:**
Right-back
**Height/Weight:**
5ft 8in/10st 12lb
**Leeds Career:**
1991–
**Leeds debut:**
As sub vs. Scunthorpe Utd (W 3–0) LC Rd. 2 (8.10.91)

Howard Wilkinson must take credit for switching young Gary to full-back, for he is ideally suited to the new wing-back role which has become common in the Premiership. A real natural talent, Gary was signed as a 17-year-old in July 1991 from Home Farm, the Dublin club which has developed so many great Irish stars over the years – Johnny Giles among them. The youngest of a family of 13 and the uncle of Ian Harte, he knows how to fend for himself, arriving as a striker and yet playing effectively as a winger – after only 15 minutes of reserve team football! – when thrown on as a substitute in the League Cup tie with Scunthorpe United.

Kelly seemed to get lost in the reserves for a while, making only two more sub appearances prior to the 1993–94 season. Equally skilful with the left or right foot, he can play on either flank and delivers a fine

**Two of the game's greatest youngsters clash as Gary Kelly challenges Ryan Giggs during the Roses match at Elland Road in April 1994. Manchester United won 2–0**

cross. But it was the decision to play him as a full-back that proved the making of him. Called into the breach left by the injured Mel Sterland, Gary not only set the Premiership alight with some exciting performances but within a year was an established international star in Jack Charlton's Republic of Ireland squad. First capped against Russia in 1994, he then featured prominently in the 1994 World Cup Finals in the USA where he was arguably Eire's most consistent competitor. He scored for the Republic in a 2–0 victory in Germany but, despite being practically ever-present in the Leeds side since August 1993, he has yet to score in the Premiership.

Gary made his 150th senior appearance in the Premiership match at Derby County on the opening day of the 1996–97 season.

# *John* **Lukic**

**John LUKIC**

**Born:**
11 December 1960, in Chesterfield
**Position:**
Goalkeeper
**Height/Weight:**
6ft 4in/13st 7lb
**Leeds Career:**
1978–1983; 1990–1996
**Leeds debut:**
vs. Valletta (W 3–0) UEFA Cup Rd. 1 L2 (3.10.79)

Now with Arsenal and about to start his 18th season in League football, John has enjoyed an illustrious career which has seen him win every honour in the book apart from a full England cap.

And he hasn't had it easy either, with some determined opposition for that coveted jersey. Having joined Leeds straight from school the young John had first to see off David Seaman at Elland Road and then fill the shoes of the popular David Harvey.

He got his break in a UEFA Cup tie in October 1979, and after replacing Harvey in the League side at Brighton that same month and keeping a clean sheet in a 0–0 draw, John went on to set a club record with 146 successive League appearances. The sequence would have continued but he asked for a transfer, as he yearned to join a successful club, and was unceremoniously dropped.

Arsenal assessed the England Youth and Under-21 international as an ideal candidate and in July 1983 laid out £125,000 to bring him to Highbury. John took over from the legendary Pat Jennings in November 1984 and grew in stature with every game, eventually sharing in Arsenal's greatest post-war period under manager George Graham.

**John Lukic, a model of consistency, set a club record number of successive appearances**

John made 223 League appearances for the Gunners and set a record by conceding only 36 goals in his first Championship campaign. He added League Cup medals to his collection – a winners' in 1987 when Arsenal beat Liverpool, a runners'-up the following year when they lost to Luton – and was rewarded with England "B" selection.

Lukic became United's most expensive import when he returned to Elland Road for £1 million in 1990 and fulfilled a dream by helping Leeds win the League title in 1992, achieving 19 shut-outs that season and conceding just 37 goals.

The tallest custodian ever to guard the Leeds fortress, John's performance slipped in 1993–94 when his handling was not as secure as usual and he lost his place to Mark Beeney. He regained his form, but rejoined Arsenal in July 1996 on a free transfer as cover for his old rival David Seaman.

# *Gary* McAllister

**Gary McALLISTER**

**Born:**
25 December 1964, at Motherwell, Lanarkshire
**Position:**
Midfield
**Height/Weight:**
5ft 10in/12st 5lb
**Leeds Career:**
1990–1996
**Leeds debut:**
vs. Everton (W 3–2) Div. 1 (25.8.90)

A classy play-maker with a Scottish international pedigree, McAllister seems to glide across the turf with the greatest of ease. He has the ability to dictate the game, and besides reading the play exceptionally well and being able to pinpoint accurate long passes Gary also packs a lethal shot and is quite useful with his heading.

**Gary McAllister shows the poise that makes him such an outstanding midfield general. He captained both Leeds and Scotland**

It all started for Gary with the Fir Park Boys' Club before Motherwell took him on in 1982. Three years later he was the proud owner of a Scottish first division championship medal but had no time to dwell on his success, for he immediately moved south to sign for Leicester City with his team-mate Ali Mauchlen.

There he gained a reputation as a scoring midfield player and won the first of his Scottish caps against East Germany in April 1990. McAllister was outstanding for Scotland in the European Championship Finals in Sweden in 1992 and again four years later in Euro '96, his only blemish a penalty kick against England, brilliantly saved by David Seaman.

After six years at Filbert Street Gary was out of contract and eager to move to a bigger club. Unimpressed by Brian Clough's abrasive approach, he rejected Nottingham Forest and settled for Leeds who stumped up a tribunal-set fee of £1 million.

The lanky Scot settled in straight away, fusing superbly with Gordon Strachan, David Batty and Gary Speed to create a class act good enough to steer United to the League Championship in 1992.

Gary succeeded Strachan as captain of club and country. It is an achievement of which he is very proud, and he fulfilled a dream when he led United out for the 1996 Coca-Cola Cup Final against Aston Villa. "It is a special feeling to captain a team at Wembley," he says. "I regarded it as one of the biggest honours of my career."

Alas, he was not to hold the cup on high as a winner: but Gary can look back on his career with some satisfaction, even if he has fewer trophies to display than many less-gifted players.

When Gary played well Leeds played well, such was his influence on the game and team. David Pleat is a great admirer and notes: "At Elland Road Gary established himself as one of the most complete midfield players in the business. He does the lot. He can track people and do the defensive business as well as being an excellent link player.

"When I inherited him at Leicester he was playing as a wide right midfielder. I stuck him in the central role and gave him more responsibility. He has developed into a super player."

Leeds fans were stunned when in July 1996 Gary decided to join Coventry City. The Sky Blues had to fork out £3 million for the privilege, and were pleased with the purchase, but it left Leeds with an awfully big hole to fill.

# *Nigel* **Martyn**

**Nigel MARTYN**

**Born:**
11 August 1966, at St Austell, Cornwall
**Position:**
Goalkeeper
**Height/Weight:**
6ft 1in/14st 7lb
**Leeds Career:**
1996–
**Leeds debut:**
vs. Derby County (3–3) Prem (17.8.96)

One of United's four major signings in the summer of 1996, Nigel was widely regarded as the best goalkeeper outside the Premiership when Leeds coughed up a record £2.25 million to prise him away from Crystal Palace in London. As it transpired, the jovial Cornishman proved to be one of the best in the Premiership too, and well worthy of his recall to the England squad.

He might be fourth in Glenn Hoddle's queue behind Seaman, Walker and Flowers, but really his form for Leeds in his first Premiership season was nothing short of inspiring.

In his first 37 games Nigel kept an incredible 19 clean sheets, a 50 percent record that no other custodian in the country came anywhere near to equalling. Such was his prowess that he conceded only one goal at Elland Road between January and May 1997.

His first club was Heavy Transport FC in the Cornish port of Par, near St Austell. Nigel then moved up to the Jewson South-Western League with St Blazey; and it was while playing in a friendly against Bristol Rovers that he was spotted. Rovers manager Gerry Francis needed only 20 minutes to decide the young custodian had a future in the game.

Nigel went on to make 101 League appearances for Bristol Rovers before Crystal Palace made him the first £1 million goalkeeper, and at the end of his first season at Selhurst Park he played a heroic game in the FA Cup Final against Manchester United. Palace held the Reds to 3–3 before losing the replay.

England Under-21 honours came Nigel's way, followed by involvement with the "B" team, including a 0–0 draw in Algeria. Graham Taylor elevated Nigel to senior international level against the CIS and gave him a game in Detroit during that disastrous US Cup fiasco. England had lost to the USA and Nigel replaced Chris Woods for the final game against Germany, which was lost 2–1.

The move to Leeds has reopened his international career and there is a widely-held opinion that Martyn is in contention for one of those three World Cup places in France.

**Nigel Martyn, probably the best goalkeeper ever to wear the Leeds jersey, in August 1997**

The Cornish shot-stopper has a superstition: he likes to come out of the tunnel second. But as far as Leeds fans are concerned, Nigel Martyn is way out in front as number one; the supporters voted him their Player of the Year in 1997.

# *David* **O'Leary**

**David O'LEARY**

**Born:**
2 May 1958, at Stoke Newington, London
**Position:**
Central defender
**Height/Weight:**
6ft 2in/12st 6lb
**Leeds Playing Career:**
1993–1995
**Leeds debut:**
vs. Manchester City (1–1) Prem (14.8.93)

Born in London but brought up in Dublin, David played for Shelbourne Juniors and had unsuccessful trials with Manchester United before joining the ranks of Arsenal's apprentices in the summer of 1973. It was a marriage made in heaven: David was to spend 20 years at Highbury, setting a club record of 558 League appearances and amassing 68 caps for the Republic of Ireland.

Howard Wilkinson turned to David in July 1993 as he wanted an experienced player to assist rookie defenders Jon Newsome and David Wetherall – and they don't come more experienced than O'Leary. The Arsenal legend was 35 when he joined Leeds on a three-year contract, but his limbs could not cope and he was forced to retire from playing with Achilles tendon trouble after just 10 games.

His name was thrown into the ring of prospective managers to take over the Eire team when Jack Charlton retired, but instead he stayed on at Elland Road as George Graham's assistant.

David O'Leary makes one of his few appearances for Leeds. This was a 1–1 draw with Manchester City in August 1993

# *Carlton* **Palmer**

**Carlton PALMER**

**Born:**
5 Dec 1965 at Oldbury
**Position:**
Central defender/midfield
**Height/Weight:**
6ft 2in/11st 10lb
**Leeds Career:**
1994–
**Leeds debut:**
vs. West Ham Utd (0–0) Prem (20.8.94)

A confident young man, Carlton Palmer took England selection in his stride when first introduced to the senior international game by Graham Taylor, who used him during the European Championship Finals in Sweden in 1992. He now has 18 caps.

His long legs make him difficult to pass and his telescopic tackle has frustrated many an opponent. Equipped with the lungs of a marathon runner, Carlton loves to surge forward from deep positions when the opportunities allow.

Palmer came into football on the YTS in 1983, learning his trade as a midfielder at Ron Atkinson's West Bromwich Albion, and then went on to skipper the England Under-21 side (four caps). He followed Atkinson to Sheffield Wednesday in 1989 where he became captain and was successfully used as a central defender.

Having missed Wednesday's League Cup Final win over Manchester United in 1991 through injury, Carlton led Wednesday in the FA Cup Final in 1993 when for the second time that season the Owls lost to the Gunners in a major domestic final.

In the summer of 1994 Wilkinson splashed out £2.6 million to add him to his squad and played Carlton mainly in midfield.

He doesn't score many goals, but when he does hit the net it is usually something special. He has taken over the captain's armband following McAllister's departure, and his enthusiasm is contagious.

**Confident Carlton Palmer takes the game to Coventry during United's Premiership game at Highfield Road in September 1996**

Pakard Bell
puma

# *Ian* **Rush**

**Ian RUSH**

**Born:**
20 October 1961, at St Asaph
**Position:**
Striker
**Height/Weight:**
6ft 0in/12st 6lb
**Leeds Career:**
1996-1997
**Leeds debut:**
vs. Derby County (3–3) Prem (17.8.96)

A goalscoring legend since joining Liverpool from Chester for £300,000 in 1980, Ian moved to Leeds in the summer of 1996 on a free transfer after 15 years and 14 major honours at Anfield. The Welsh international (73 caps) scored 14 League goals for Chester, 139 for Liverpool, seven with Juventus and just three with Leeds, where he experienced his driest spell. So disappointed was he that he told the manager he should drop him for the Leicester game.

George Graham refused, and explained: "I have never criticised Ian. The goals haven't come but I have nothing but admiration for his attitude and work rate." Graham was right; for the famous boots struck two goals in a 3–0 triumph over Leicester.

Rushy's glittering role of honour includes a record-breaking 346 League and Cup games for Liverpool, five championships, three FA Cups and, of course, the European Cup in 1984. That season he netted 48 goals and was crowned Player of the Year by both the PFA and the Football Writers.

Rush has never been content with just passing statistical landmarks such as Roger Hunt's Liverpool scoring record, Denis Law's FA Cup total and Geoff Hurst's League Cup tally. Stark statistics are merely the skeleton of his success: they don't reveal the meat – the quality of the great goal-scorer who scores great goals, although his season at Leeds was not one of his best.

**Goalscoring legend Ian Rush ran out of ammunition in his single season at Elland Road before his Newcastle transfer. In this FA Cup third-round replay, Leeds beat Crystal Palace 1–0: Rod Wallace scored**

**Lee Sharpe gets the better of former colleague Nicky Butt in the game at Elland Road in September 1996. But it was Manchester United's day – they won 4–0!**

# *Lee* Sharpe

**Lee SHARPE**

**Born:**
27 May 1971, at Halesowen
**Position:**
Midfield
**Height/Weight:**
6ft/11st
**Leeds Career:**
1996–
**Leeds debut:**
vs. Derby (3–3) Prem (17.8.96)

There was a lot of excitement when Leeds invested a record £4.5 million for the young Manchester United star in the 1996 close season, but we have still to see the best of him.

Lee made his debut as a full-back with Torquay United when he was 16, and within a year was on the Manchester United payroll following a £185,000 swoop, notching up a total of 193 League appearances and 21 goals for the Reds.

He was voted PFA Young Player of the Year in 1991, the year in which he won the first of his eight England caps.

# *Gary* Speed

**Gary SPEED**

**Born:**
8 September 1969 at Mancot, North Wales
**Position:**
Forward
**Height/Weight:**
6ft/12st
**Leeds Career:**
1996–1997
**Leeds debut:**
vs. Oldham Ath (0–0) Div. 2 (6.5.89)

A left-sided player who is effective on the flank, in midfield or defence and good in the air, Gary came up through the ranks to establish a reputation as a goal-scoring left-winger towards the close of the second-division championship campaign.

Gary possesses a stunning shot and won the first of his 37 Welsh caps against Costa Rica in May 1990. He also has genuine pace and was at his best in the 1992 championship side, scoring seven goals in 41 first-division appearances.

In March 1996 a £3.4 million bid from Everton was rejected, but the deal was struck three months later.

**Gordon Strachan, the wee man with the big heart and lashings of natural skill. A model professional and Howard Wilkinson's right-hand man, Strachan went on to play for, and manage, Coventry City**

# *Gordon* **Strachan**

**Gordon STRACHAN**

**Born:**
9 February 1957, in Edinburgh
**Position:**
Midfield
**Height/Weight:**
5ft 6in/ 10st 3lb
**Leeds Career:**
1989–1995
**Leeds debut:**
vs. Portsmouth (w 1–0) Div. 2 (25.3.89)

They say one man doesn't make a team, but the contribution made to United by skipper and midfield orchestrator Gordon Strachan was colossal. An influential and inspiring general whose appetite for work is insatiable, he was the spark behind both the second division and League championship triumphs.

Gordon came into football with Dundee in 1976 and won Scottish Premiership (two), Cup (three) and ECWC medals with Aberdeen before signing for Manchester United in 1984. In nearly five years at Old Trafford, Gordon made 166 League appearances and won an FA Cup-winners' medal.

Surprisingly sold by Alex Ferguson in 1989 for a give-away £330,000, he went on to become one of Leeds United's most inspiring skippers. Capped 50 times by Scotland, whom he skippered, he played in the 1982 and 1986 World Cup Finals tournaments.

Howard Wilkinson said of him: "Gordon stayed faithful to the game, true to his profession and has not prostituted his gifts. He realised and appreciated the value of keeping his feet on the ground, being single-minded and not getting involved in the bull in which some players can become swamped."

Gordon was being groomed to take over from Wilkinson, but made a shock move to Coventry City in March 1995 after Ron Atkinson promised him the succession to the Coventry managerial chair.

**David Wetherall, a solid professional whose consistency and ability are not often appreciated by the media**

# *David* **Wetherall**

**David WETHERALL**

**Born:**
14 March 1971, Sheffield
**Position:**
Central defender
**Height/Weight:**
6ft 3in/ 13st 12lb
**Leeds Career:**
1991–
**Leeds debut:**
sub vs. Arsenal (2–2) Div.1 (3.9.91)

In his early career, David captained the England Schoolboys team and won Youth caps at Under-19. A University graduate, he completed a chemistry degree in 1992. David represented Britain in the 1991 World Student Games when the football team won a bronze medal. A trainee with Sheffield Wednesday, he moved to Leeds in 1991 along with Newsome. He has since progressed well and was voted the manager's Player of the Year in 1995–96.

# The Premiership Managers

Chapter 6

**Managers these days are personalities as big as – or sometimes bigger than – the players they have to handle.**

Since the advent of the Premiership five years ago, the men in charge of the country's leading clubs have grown in stature and importance, and now have responsibility for just about every aspect of their club – playing and coaching staff, buying and selling and media relations being the most important.

Not every manager, of course, is cut out for the job. Some are fine coaches and excellent spotters of juvenile talent. Others are expert tacticians. Some excel at man-management (ever more vital in these days of megabucks-a-year salaries to some players). Very few are capable of handling *all* those tasks – and the other time-consuming bits and pieces that need doing.

So the choice of a manager grows more and more vital at the same time as it grows more and more difficult. Few managers ever lasted long even in the days when soccer was a mere sport, not a massive business. Now, with so much at stake, the need to eliminate errors is vital: the choice of "The Boss" has become the hardest choice the board of directors ever faces.

Leeds had only had four managers between their election to the Football League and the Second World War: Dick Ray (twice), Arthur Fairclough and Bill Hampson. They had another five between 1946 and Don Revie's promotion in 1961: Willis Edwards, Frank Buckley – an early "character" of the managerial business, especially during his time at Wolves – Horatio Carter, Bill Lambton and Jack Taylor.

Revie's successful spell ended with his move to become England team manager in 1974 and led to a 14-year spell in which eight big names were tried, with little success. Brian Clough, Jimmy Armfield, Jock Stein, Jimmy Adamson and former United heroes Allan Clarke, Eddie Gray and Billy Bremner all tried and failed. Not until Howard Wilkinson arrived was Revie's ghost exorcised.

## *Howard* **Wilkinson**

Wilkinson led Leeds United into the new-style FA Premier League in 1992 as Football League champions, an achievement which not only inscribed his name forever in the club's history-books but also blew away those ghosts of the Seventies which had relentlessly haunted Elland Road.

He suggested, without a hint of false modesty, that Leeds United appointed him as manager just in the nick of time. It was Monday 10 October 1988 when he was persuaded to leave Sheffield Wednesday to take on the daunting task of revitalising the Peacocks – a brief he undertook with a brand of professional precision uncannily reminiscent of Revie himself.

Born in Sheffield on 13 November 1943, Wilkinson is not a man who displays his emotions openly. Win, lose or draw, the reaction is always controlled, his pale blue eyes, set in a poker-face, suggesting – somewhat misleadingly – a touch of aloofness, even of arrogance. Yes, he has boundless confidence in his abilities, but it is justified by his enormous knowledge and understanding of football – as I was able to learn for myself during many hours spent with him motoring across Eastern Europe on the England Under-21 team bus.

Wilkinson's analysis of the game is clinically perceptive, and yet behind his technical mastery lies a passionate obsession with and appreciation of the artistry and poetry of the game. He relates his boyhood experiences with a warm nostalgia which reawakens the past in glowibg colours. The son of a miner, he vividly recalls the Saturday-afternoon trips he and his father took together on the clanging, rocking trams that crawled their way to Hillsborough.

He can even pinpoint the precise moment he fell in love with football. Says Howard: "I'd just watched Stanley Matthews win the Cup Final for Blackpool on somebody else's TV. One family in our yard had a nine-inch set and the lads and dads were crammed around it in a room that can have been no more than nine feet by nine. Everyone was there to live the fantasy – enjoy the fairytale. It's what football is all about.

"It's the contradiction that attracts you to football. You can see your hero perform miracles on a Saturday afternoon, and then have the satisfaction of going out on the Rec to find that you can come somewhere close to it at your own level. If it was easy it wouldn't be so attractive."

Howard wore the Number Seven shirt from that day but was never able to emulate his idol, though he represented the England Grammar Schools and was an amateur with Sheffield United. He achieved good A level results, but an offer to join the junior ranks at Hillsborough put paid to plans for a degree course in civil engineering and set him on his way to a career in football.

He joined Wednesday in June 1962 and earned England Youth honours while on the books, but in four years with the Owls Howard made only 22 League appearances and did not establish himself until joining Brighton, with whom he played over 100 games in six years. It was while at the Goldstone Ground that the door opened on the career that was to be the making of him.

Howard, who was still only 22, attended a course

**Howard Wilkinson's teenage dream was to be the Stanley Matthews of Sheffield Wednesday**

**Howard WILKINSON**

**Born:**
13 November 1943, in Sheffield

**Playing career:**
1962 Sheffield Wednesday, 1966 Brighton & Hove Albion

**Honours:**
League championship 1992
League Cup finalists 1996
Promotion from Division Two 1984 (manager, Sheffield Wed)
Division Two champions 1990 (Leeds United)

**International honours:**
First player to appear for England at all levels - Schoolboy, Amateur,Youth, Under-23 and Senior (Two full caps)

**Managerial career:**
England semi-professional
England Under-21
Notts County (coach, 1981–83 manager)
Sheffield Wednesday 1983–88
Leeds United 1988–96
FA Technical Director

**"The Gaffer" relays instructions to the team from the bench**

for coaches run by Steve Burtenshaw. "I joined to fill the evenings up," he recalls, "and fell in love with it straight away. I know it sounds corny, but I wasn't bad". That has proved an understatement, for he went on to gain the full FA Coaching badge; and on leaving Brighton put his theories to the test as player-manager of Boston United, taking over as player-boss of the Northern Premier League club following the departure of his mentor Jim Smith, now manager of Derby County. Under Wilkinson's leadership, Boston won three titles.

The reputation that he forged at Boston was further enhanced by his success as the Football Association's regional coach in Sheffield. By that stage, Wilkinson had completed a degree in physical education from Sheffield University – adding more to his qualifications – and a spell in charge of the England semi-professional side was followed by an invitation from the then England boss Ron Greenwood to take control of the national Under-21 squad.

In December 1979, Notts County manager Jimmy Sirrel invited him to become his coach. County were sixth from bottom in Division Two at the time and falling fast, but by the close of the following season were bouncing into Division One. Wilkinson was promoted to team manager!

By then the clean-cut, sharp-featured Yorkshireman was acknowledged as the brightest young coach in the business, and it was no surprise when England manager Bobby Robson tried to recruit him to his permanent staff. But Wilko boldly stayed loyal to County, explaining: "If you have been in football any length of time you learn one thing: that is that it is a handicap to have an ego".

Elevation to a yet higher level was inevitable, however, and in June 1983 Wilkinson succeeded the former Leeds United legend "Big" Jack Charlton as the manager of Sheffield Wednesday, leading his home-town team back to Division One in his first season with the club.

The Owls did well under his stewardship, flying close to success in both League and Cup, but frustration at a lack of the financial resources he felt were needed to take the team a step forward probably led to his parting company with the Owls. Even so, it was quite a surprise when he quit to take on the sizeable challenge of Leeds United.

Once installed at Elland Road, Wilkinson spent big and often, yet warned: "The mere acquisition of high-priced footballers with big reputations guarantees nothing." In this case it guaranteed a return to Division One after an absence of eight years.

Mind you, in the process United won few friends outside of the West Riding; but in answer to charges that they were dour and ruthless, Wilkinson replied: "You have to be realistic. It seems to me that the objective of management is to perform the task that the directors outline. It was the unanimous wish of the Leeds United directors to get out of the second division. That is what we did.

"I don't understand those critics who claim to know my philosophy of the game by judging me on one season. I looked at the task, dealt with it, and accomplished the objective. People look for what is not there all the time. As a second-division club, you are not going to be able to attract too many first-division players; so why do they expect you to play first-division football with second-division footballers?"

Wilkinson has always been able to cut through the flannel and deal with basic realities. The fact that he has won titles while playing a long-ball game sometimes seems like a millstone around his neck. Naturally he resents suggestions that he does not advocate the "beautiful" game, for no one appreciates the finer points more than he does. His reasoning is sound, and responds to circumstances. He brought in hard men such as Vinnie Jones and Chris Kamara to help United haul themselves out of Division Two; then, when the stage was set, he introduced real pass-masters in the shape of little Gordon Strachan and Gary McAllister.

**Getting the message across. Wilkinson is respected as one of our foremost coaches**

After finishing fourth in their first season back in the top flight, United shook the establishment by winning the League Championship, squeezing Manchester United out in a thrilling climax. Howard Wilkinson walked on water as far as the fans and directors were concerned. He had a job at Elland Road for life.

Alas, troubled times lay ahead. Despite enhancing the quality of the playing staff by introducing immense talents such as Eric Cantona, Gary McAllister, Tony Yeboah, Tomas Brolin and goalkeeper Nigel Martyn, Wilkinson saw the winning formula evaporate, although Leeds were Coca-Cola Cup finalists in 1996. A 3–0 defeat by Aston Villa at Wembley only fuelled the unrest; and when Leslie Silver relinquished the chair, the clouds over Wilkinson's office became decidedly blacker. When the fizz went out of the Coca-Cola Cup team, he decided on dramatic surgery. The arrival of new owners appeared to offer sufficient funds for rebuilding, but the process stalled as the take-over was challenged in the courts, and Leeds got the 1996–97 season off to a stuttering start.

A 4–0 home humiliation inflicted by arch-rivals Manchester United in the first week of September 1996 hastened the inevitable, and Howard Wilkinson was sacked two days later. He said he was "sad and shocked" at the decision as he contemplated the end of his eight-year reign – a reign on which he could look back with some pride, with a string of exciting youngsters in the fold and the team in the top division. He had not only given Leeds United back their self-respect by winning two championships and reaching a cup final, but left the club in a much stronger position than he had found it. Even after that defeat by Manchester United, Leeds were ninth in the FA Carling Premiership – as Wilkinson pointed out, with a flash of his familiar tartness.

Wilkinson's sword now cuts a new dash following his appointment as Technical Director of the Football Association on January 6, 1997. Always highly-respected in the corridors of power, Howard had been part of Bobby Robson's technical team in the 1990 World Cup Finals in Italy, watching and briefing on England's opponents; and on his new appointment, leading figures in football proclaimed him the saviour of the English game, with Glenn Hoddle, Alex Ferguson, Graham Kelly and Gordon Taylor among those giving glowing tributes. His major brief to develop youth football in this country makes it potentially the most powerful job in English football.

Wilkinson should be well-suited to the challenge. As down-to-earth as a pitman's shovel, he has never lost touch with his roots. Only too well aware of his limitations and the adverse criticism levelled at him by the Press, he told me once: "People are always looking for what's not there. I don't find the media attention difficult – I quite enjoy it – but with them, football management has become a personality business, and with the best will in the world I can't see me becoming a personality. The game is not about making statues, or monuments anyway; it's greater than that – greater than any individual."

Despite his public image, Wilkinson is a warm family man with a sharp sense of humour and an ear for music. A meal with the family, a glass of wine and a handsome cigar is his way of switching off from the tensions of football. Behind the veneer is a strong sense of humour – he is a hilarious mimic. During his days at Hillsborough, if you rang him on his private line he would answer: "Yorkshire Electricity Board".

## *George* **Graham**

Within hours of Wilkinson's departure George Graham was returned to football management after a 19-month enforced sabbatical.

Outwardly, nothing had changed since Graham was axed by Arsenal and subsequently banned by the FA for a year for allegedly accepting illegal payments from a Norwegian agent. The confident Scot, who had always pleaded his innocence, still hungered for a piece of the action.

"I've relaxed a bit more, especially with the media", said Graham, two weeks after turning down the opportunity to manage Manchester City. "What was important was to come back to a job that gave me the best opportunity for success".

According to then-Leeds chairman Bill Fotherby the reasons for Graham's ban were discussed but discounted, and he was offered the managerial seat simply on the grounds that he was the best man available for the job.

At 51, George was starting again from scratch. The man who made the Gunners great again still feels betrayed by Arsenal, the club he restored to glory. Indeed, such were his accomplishments at Highbury that he now stands alongside the immortal names of Chapman, Busby, Cullis and Shankly in the fables of football management; yet he knows that history will count for nothing should he not deliver the silverware to the Leeds United trophy cabinet.

A distinguished figure, always immaculately groomed, on one visit to meet him at Highbury I swear that the famous bust of Herbert Chapman acknowledged his presence with a wink as we passed through the marble hall. Certainly Arsenal's most revered manager – who, incidentally, managed Leeds City between 1912 and 1919 when the illegal payments scandal led to City's expulsion from the League – would have approved of Graham's moral stand following an unfortunate fracas between the players of Arsenal and Manchester United. The manager took full responsibility for the behaviour of his players and solemnly accepted a fine of two weeks' wages, which I understand was enforced at his own suggestion.

Graham sees it as his responsibility to bring his influence to bear wherever he can "in a right and proper manner". A fiercely-ambitious man, his aim at Highbury was to build a dynasty of success in keeping with the halcyon days of the 1930s; and this, to his credit, he did. Pride is an integral part of his make-up: easily riled by criticism of his team or his methods, he was extremely anxious to rid Arsenal of the "boring" tag first stuck on them back in the Chapman era which, like the "lucky Arsenal" label, had never really gone away.

His initial year in charge of Arsenal was most encouraging, with a Littlewoods Cup Final win over Liverpool providing an earlier-than-expected reward. A year later the Gunners were back at Wembley to defend the trophy, but this time were turned over good and proper by little Luton Town.

Then came the ultimate prize; the first division championship, clinched in the most dramatic fashion with a last-gasp goal at Anfield. Yet far from being a climax to his managerial career, Graham saw this as the beginning of something great. It was, too; and his final tally of triumphs in nine years at Highbury was: two League championships; the FA Cup; two League

Cups; and the European Cup-Winners' Cup.

George has two major passions outside his work: his garden and an insatiable fascination with the past history of the game. When all is said and done, he was only the fifth manager to lead the Gunners to a League championship; yet an achievement which gave him even deeper satisfaction was to join Bill Nicholson (Tottenham Hotspur), Howard Kendall (Everton), Bob Paisley and Kenny Dalglish (Liverpool) in that select band of men who have played for a championship-winning team, then gone on to manage the same club to further title success.

George "Stroller" Graham had been a key figure in Arsenal's triumphant side of the early Seventies. He was in the team which defeated Anderlecht in the European Fairs Cup Final in 1970, putting the first trophy on the Highbury sideboard for 17 years, and then figured prominently in that wonderful League and FA Cup double-winning combination in 1971.

**Manager George Graham demonstrates the skills which made him a legend in his playing days**

**George GRAHAM**

**Born:**
30 November 1944, in Bargeddie

**Playing career:**
Aston Villa
Chelsea
Arsenal
Manchester United
Portsmouth
Crystal Palace

**Honours:**
Scotland (12 caps)
League Cup 1965 (player)
FA Cup 1971 (player), 1993 (manager)
League Championship 1971 (player) 1989, 1991 (manager)
League Cup 1987, 1993 (manager)
Promotion from Division Three 1985 (manager)
European Cup-Winners' Cup 1994 (manager)

**Managerial career:**
Crystal Palace (coach)
Millwall 1984–86
Arsenal 1986–95
Leeds United 1996–97

A striker of inspirational imagination and delicate skills, his seemingly leisurely approach was very misleading. During the mid-Sixties the tall, elegant Graham had impressed his subtle touch on the Chelsea forward line after arriving at Stamford Bridge from Villa Park in a £5,000 transfer in June 1964. He developed a telepathic rapport with Barry Bridges, after making a scoring debut for the Blues against Sunderland, and in a team propelled by the midfield mastery of Terry Venables and Johnny Hollins, "Stroller" claimed 46 goals in just over two seasons before moving to Highbury in September 1966 in exchange for Tommy Baldwin and £75,000.

George's ability on the ball, his vision and accuracy in passing inevitably saw him withdrawn to a midfield role before completing his playing career with Manchester United (43 League appearances); Portsmouth (61 League appearances) and Crystal Palace (44 League appearances), where he finally ended up playing centre-half with the reserves.

In all, George Graham scored 59 League goals in 277 games for Arsenal – including eight appearances as substitute – and racked up a total of 105 goals in an overall playing career of 444 (11) games. Capped a

**Graham returns to Highbury for the first time as Leeds United's manager in October 1996**

dozen times by Scotland, having previously been honoured at Schoolboy, Youth and Under-23 levels, he also collected runners'-up awards in the League Cup in 1963, 1968 and 1969 and in the FA Cup in 1972.

It was Terry Venables who kept George in football when, at the age of 35, battered, bruised and feeling worse for wear following years of physical abuse to his body (including a broken leg and broken ankle) George was contemplating taking on a pub on the South Coast. Graham had coached the Crystal Palace reserve team for Venables, and jumped at the opportunity to work for his former boss managing the youth team at Loftus Road.

At QPR, having to work within a budget provided an invaluable grounding for the years ahead; and in December 1982, when Millwall found themselves in trouble, it was the canny Scot to whom they turned for help. He didn't disappoint, even though he had taken over a team needing to win 12 of its last 15 games to survive in Division Three. Survive they did, and within six years the Lions were roaring as never before as they gained promotion to the first division for the first time in their history. By then George had vacated Cold Blow Lane for the stately home of Highbury; but it was his work and organisation on which this ultimate success was founded.

"I learned an awful lot in three-and-a-half years at Millwall," reflected George. "It was probably the equivalent of managing another club for 10 years, there was so much to take in. I think I was good for Millwall and Millwall was good for me. It was a very strong partnership and I was quite proud of what I did there."

When Graham arrived at Highbury in May 1986, Arsenal were £1.24 million in debt: not an outstanding amount at today's values, but a significant overdraft at the time, particularly as the North London giants were seen as one of the more affluent clubs in the Football League. Success over the following four seasons generated £9 million-plus in revenue, not only wiping out the deficit and paying the club's mounting running costs, but providing a healthy profit as well. Big money was invested on new players, but George is a shrewd operator and his returns from selling unwanted talent meant that in real terms his outgoings were very conservative.

Graham's reputation for getting things right was growing; and though Arsenal's failure to retain that first League title under his stewardship prompted the usual trite criticism from certain quarters, he adamantly refuted accusations of being "The Great Dictator." One former Arsenal star did dub him "Colonel Ghadaffi", it is true, but this was a remark made more in jest than in fear.

George laughs at suggestions that he runs a draconian régime. He says: "I have been labelled a disciplinarian but I think it is the wrong word. I would say I am a very professional person. If other people want to put their words to it that is fine, but my interpretation would be that I expect standards to be met.

"When I was a player I experienced different ways of management. There were no strict standards at Chelsea when I was there. We had a lot of youngsters and they were a very good side, an excellent team. Then I went to Arsenal where it was much more organised – there was greater discipline about the place. I picked up things from a lot of people and have put my own slant on my experiences and come up with what I believe is the way to manage.

"I worked under some good people like Terry Venables, Don Howe, Dave Sexton and Bertie Mee. Even playing alongside Frank McLintock was a tremendous education. They all have different strengths, so it is just a matter of putting them all together, wrapping them up and coming out with one product.

"Everybody learns from other people: believe me, I don't know anybody who has come up with a totally original idea, I really don't. Everything in this game has been done before."

George is never more at home than when on the training field. He says: "I enjoy coaching very much. I like working with players. Then after wearing my coaching hat in the morning, I try to don my managerial cap in the afternoon. Yes, at times it is difficult, but I'm a great believer in facts in life, and it is a fact that there are teachers and there are doers. I like coaching but I want to be remembered always as a doer."

The youngest of six, George knew hardship from the beginning. George was born in Bargeddie in 1946, and was only two weeks old when his father died of tuberculosis; but the struggles his family experienced then have made him more appreciative of his rewards today. They certainly shaped his outlook on life. It was then that he had to stand up for himself, and today's self-assured posture, which to some gives him an air almost of arrogance, is merely an extension of the young George's tough outer shell.

A dapper dresser, George strives to be the best at everything and for the most part has succeeded grandly, in a career which lifted him from the outskirts of Glasgow to a mock-Georgian home in stylish Hertfordshire and now to the pleasures of the West Riding. Yet George's playing and managerial careers seem to offer a distinct contradiction in terms. In those distant playing days, George pulled almost every stroke in the book to ensure as easy a life as possible. It could be because he's been there, done it all, and knows what players can get away with when given an inch that he now rules Elland Road with such authority.

With £10 million at his disposal, he stressed, he would not be rushing out to sign players for Leeds. At first the results did not come and the new manager's priority was to sort out a defence that gave far too much away.

By the turn of the year Leeds United were boasting one of the meanest defences in the country, and from these foundations Graham intends turning on the style in 1997–98.

Wilkinson and Graham are of course the only Leeds managers who have been involved in the Premiership, George being in fact the 18th manager hired by the club since its formation as Leeds United in 1920.

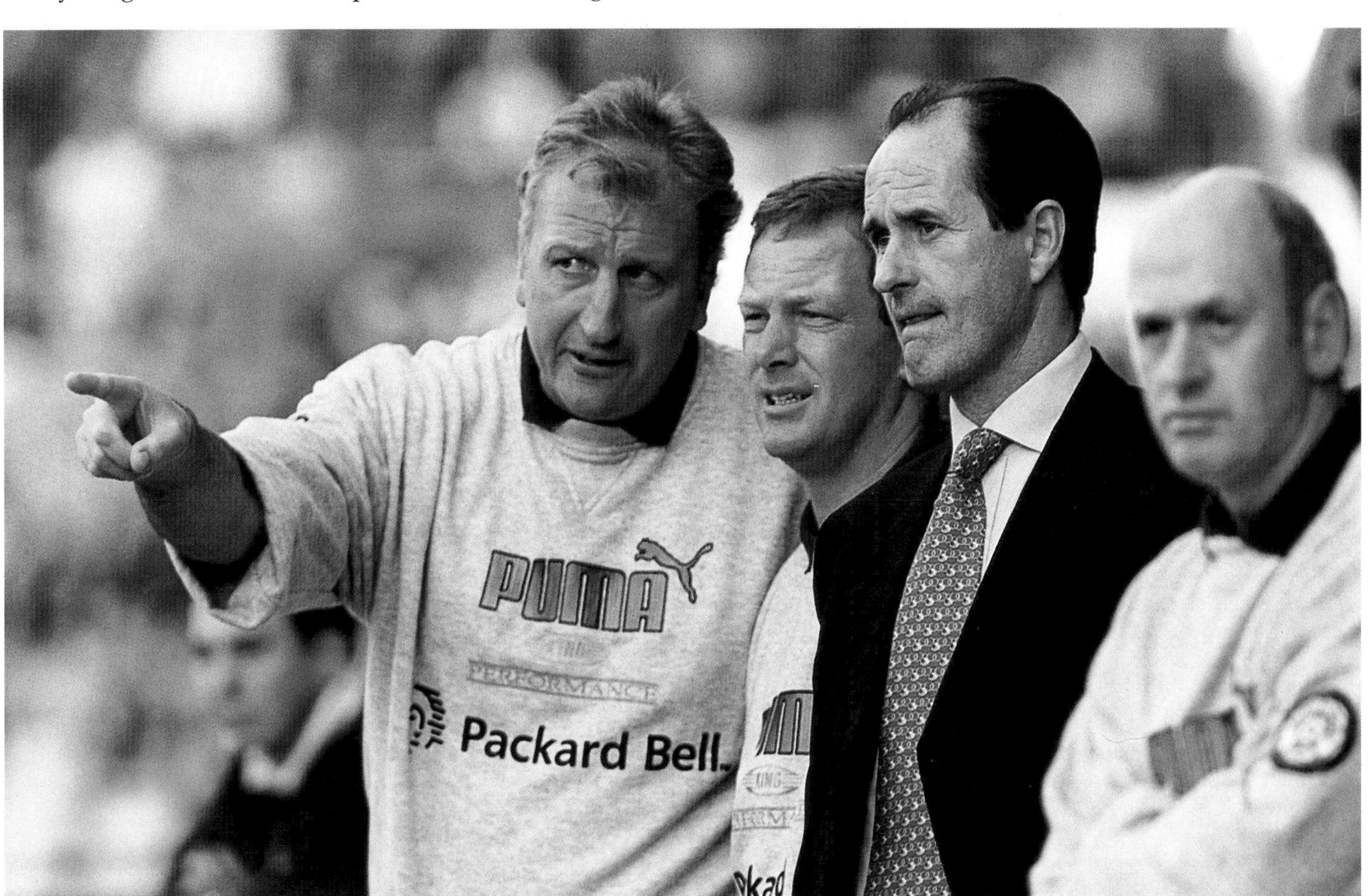


**The men who know: Graham talks tactics with his coaching team during a 1996 game vs. Coventry**

# Chapter 7

# Leeds' Foreign Stars

**Long before the Bosman Ruling, United was taking full advantage of the skills and insights overseas players bring to the English game.**

There are two schools of thought regarding the employment of foreign players in English football. Some believe that foreigners bring additional skill and vision to the game and thus broaden our horizons by offering a passport to greatness. Others, led by PFA chief executive Gordon Taylor, claim the legions from abroad are a considerable threat to the home guard.

There are merits in both arguments, but I'm reminded of a conversation I once had with that great BBC radio commentator Bryon Butler, who recalled Enzo Bearzot, the old charmer who led Italy to the World Cup championship in 1982, claiming he knew why England were under-achievers in international football. "Too many foreigners", he insisted.

Bearzot meant the Scots, Welsh and Irish, who have infiltrated League football to a very great degree since the beginning of professionalism; but to which, thanks to the Bosman ruling, may now be added names from all quarters of the globe.

Perhaps Leeds United have been better able than some to maintain a happy medium in this respect. Foreign players are no strangers to Elland Road. In the Sixties, we used to thrill to the mesmerising magic of that great South African left-winger Albert Johanneson, the first coloured player to appear in an FA Cup Final at Wembley, when Leeds lost to Liverpool in extra time in 1965. Poor Albert was tragically found dead in a council tower-block flat, where he had spent his last lonely years as a confirmed alcoholic. "Yoyo" was only 53. He was a one-off, of course, whereas in the changing climate of the 1990s it is not out of the ordinary for a team to field more foreign

**Tomas Brolin makes one of his rare appearances**

players than British ones.

Maybe this is not always a bad thing, especially if you believe one of the stand-up comics who performed at the "evening of football comedy" staged in December 1994 by Carling, sponsors of the Premiership. "I'll tell you why foreigners beat us at football. They have Marco Van Basten. We have David Batty. They have Gianluca Vialli. We have David Platt". Of course.

The irony is that it has all changed around now, and Leeds have kept abreast of the times by complementing their squad with a fair sprinkling of more colourful names.

# *Tomas* **Brolin**

It must be said that Leeds have not enjoyed overwhelming success with their foreign imports. Tomas Brolin, signed like Tony Yeboah for £4.5 million by Wilkinson, looked the business after eye-catching performances against Manchester United and Bolton, despite having played only three games for Parma and four more for Sweden in six months. He was supposed to form the cutting edge of the attack alongside Yeboah, but neither player was fit enough or around long enough to make it work.

The Swede, who came to the fore during the 1992 European Championship Finals in his home country as a striker, had an unhappy time in Yorkshire and regarded his failure to make the starting-line at Wembley in the Coca-Cola Cup Final (he came on for the last 25 minutes) as sufficient reason for exercising an "escape" option in his contract. He spent part of the 1996–97 season on loan in Switzerland, but during the summer manager Graham held out an olive-branch and he agreed to return. Brolin was knocked off course, however, by a bird which flew into his windscreen *en route* to the airport.

**Tomas BROLIN**

**Born:** 29 November 1969
**Birthplace:** Harmsosand, Sweden
**Position**: Forward
**Ht:** 5ft 9in
**Wt: 12st 2lb**
**Signed for Leeds:**
25 November 1995, for £4.5 million, from Parma
**Former clubs:**
Sundsvall, Norrköping (Swe), Parma (Ita), Leeds United
**Leeds record:**
17 apps, 2 goals
**Honours:**
54 Swedish caps
1992 Italian Cup
1993 European Cup-Winners' Cup
1996 Coca-Cola Cup finalist

# *Eric* **Cantona**

Eric Cantona was the cult hero of the West Riding when the Premiership opened its doors. Howard Wilkinson had made a brave stand, underpinned by a £900,000 investment, to bring the controversial striker to these shores.

The enigmatic French international first came to our attention in January 1992 when, during a self-imposed retirement, he began a week's trial at Hillsborough. Sheffield Wednesday were trying to arrange a loan deal with his club, Nantes. Cantona had threatened to give up the game when the French FA doubled a one-month suspension after he verbally abused the disciplinary committee which banned him. This was just one episode in a troubled history which had followed him from Nice, Auxerre, Martigues (on loan), Marseilles, Bordeaux (again on loan), Montpellier, who got rid of him after a nasty business with a team-mate, and Nîmes.

**Eric CANTONA**

**Born:** 24 May 1966
**Birthplace:** Nîmes, France
**Position**: Forward
**Ht:** 6ft 2in
**Wt:** 14st 3lb
**Signed for Leeds:**
6 February 1992, for £900,000, from Nîmes
**Former clubs:**
Nice (Fra), Auxerre (Fra), Martigues (Fra, loan), Marseilles (Fra), Bordeaux, (Fra, loan), Montpellier (Fra), Nîmes (Fra),
1992 Leeds United
**Leeds record:**
66 apps, 32 goals

**Honours:**
45 French caps
1992 League Championship
1993, 1994, 1996, 1997 Premiership
1994, 1996 FA Cup

Cantona was banned from international football for a year by the French authority after lambasting national team boss Henri Michel in 1988; disciplined twice in one season for making gestures to the crowd; sent off for throwing the ball at a referee; and also involved in fights with team-mates at Auxerre. He really was the bad boy of French football. But Wednesday were willing to give him a chance, and thought they had him in the bag.

It was quite a surprise when he refused to stay for a second week and returned to France. Wednesday boss Trevor Francis had not seen him play on grass because the ground was frozen, and wanted to make sure. Cantona was of the opinion that he did not have to prove himself. Howard Wilkinson had obviously been monitoring the situation and knew a player when he saw one. He reacted instantly, agreeing a loan deal with Nîmes that brought Cantona to Leeds.

Eric made his debut as a substitute at Oldham on

8 February, 1992, and made his first start at Everton (1–1) in the very next fixture, played on the 23rd. It tells you something about his charisma when you realise that by the end of that Championship-winning season he was the darling of the crowd, the "Ooh-ah Cantona" refrain now established as a signature tune for Leeds United. Yet of the 15 first division games in which Cantona was involved, he started in only six.

Michel Platini, one of the greatest French players of all time, regarded Cantona as among the top 10 strikers in Europe, believing he was a genius but had yet to prove it at club level. He joked that Cantona would have been in danger of "becoming a bum" had he rejected Leeds and insisted on staying in retirement. As for the man himself, he suggested: "English football is less technical and more physical, but it will suit me".

Of solid build, Cantona's six-foot-two frame was always imposingly erect. There was a definite arrogance in his body language, as if he knew he belonged on a different sporting plane. Cantona looked like what he was. He didn't run – at least not in the accepted sense, like you or me: he didn't charge, scurry or scamper after the ball. What he did was far more exciting and graceful than that.

English strikers are so predictable. Eric brought an element of surprise, with delicate flicks and pushes. He was a throwback to those cavalier days when the philosophy of soccer's princes was to entertain as well as win.

Eric scored his first goal in English football in the 2–0 home victory over Luton Town at the end of February. He notched up another in the 5–1 demolition of Wimbledon and hit the target again in the 3–0 defeat of Chelsea. He was granted only six minutes in this game; but then that was all he needed.

Twice Cantona bamboozled Chelsea defender Paul Elliott as he flicked the ball over his head, gathered it again in his stride, flicked it up a couple of times as if messing around on the training pitch, juggled for an opening and – still giving no signs of the explosion to come – steadied himself as if pondering where to make the next play. Then, without any warning to goalkeeper David Beasant, he unleashed a mighty drive that sent the ball hurtling past the astonished custodian like a ballistic missile.

Other pros could only stand in awe. "You have to applaud ability like that", commented Elliot gracefully. "It was just quality and so is he. Very, very talented. That goal was simply marvellous. I can honestly say I haven't seen anything like it since I played in Italy and then it came from Marco Van Basten. That should tell you everything."

Even that touch of magic did not win Eric a place in the starting line until the opening game of the next season, but it certainly got the message across to the fans.

Eric was to make 12 (1) Premiership appearances and score six goals, three of them in a memorable 5–0 drubbing of Tottenham. Wilkinson dropped him at the end of October as he struggled to find a winning combination. The Frenchman didn't like it and the rumbles of disenchantment began to get louder. Then came the news of his transfer to Manchester United. Leeds fans were stunned.

Cantona claimed Howard Wilkinson had driven him out. He alleged in his book *Cantona - My Story*: "It became more and more clear he wanted to get rid of me. It was a well-planned move by him. The supporters were confused and did not know who they should believe".

Wilko responded: "His claims against me and Leeds United are factually incorrect and I can prove that".

The war of words continued following the £1.1 million transfer. The United players had realised Eric's days were numbered. Lee Chapman claimed: "After our European Cup defeat by Rangers, Eric was dropped for the subsequent game against QPR, but the team was not announced until the morning of the match, when we gathered to rehearse our set-piece plays.

"As was the normal practice at Leeds, those not in the starting line-up were handed red bibs and required to act as the opposition; players were not always told of their fall from grace beforehand, and quite often the first a player knew of it was when the coach, Mick Hennigan, thrust the dreaded bib in his direction.

"To say Eric was not thrilled would be an understatement. On our return to the hotel he ignored two attempts at conversation by the manager. He also failed to turn up for the pre-match meal and arrived late for the subsequent team meeting wearing the kind of clothes I knew would antagonise the manager. Eric was given a public dressing-down and told to make his journey to Paris immediately."

Nothing is ever entirely black-and-white, and there is no doubt that Eric's off-the-cuff football was not totally in tune with the more direct style of Leeds. His inclusion demanded compromise from both player and team, and neither was best served. The *enfant terrible* of French football would go on to more glory and controversy at Old Trafford.

**Gunnar Halle: a George Graham signing who settled in at once and shows bags of promise**

# *Gunnar* **Halle**

Gunnar Halle's £400,000 move from Oldham Athletic in December 1996 went almost unnoticed outside West Yorkshire. Yet this scoop by George Graham could prove a real bargain, for the 54-times-capped Norwegian international seemed at home at United immediately he arrived.

**Gunnar HALLE**

**Born:** 11 August 1965
**Birthplace:** Oslo, Norway
**Position**: Defender
**Ht:** 5ft 11in
**Wt:** 11st 2lb
**Signed for Leeds:**
12 December 1996, for £400,000, from Oldham Athletic
**Former clubs:**
Lillestrom (Nor),
Oldham Athletic, Leeds United
**Leeds record:**
23 apps, 0 goals
**Honours:**
54 Norwegian caps,
1991 Division 2 championship

# *Phil* **Masinga**

Phil Masinga proved less of a success. The South African international striker, who cost £275,000 from Mamelode Sundowns in August 1994, was subsequently booted out by the Department of Employment for not playing in the required 75 per cent of games.

**Phil MASINGA**

**Born:** 28 June 1969
**Birthplace:** Johannesburg, South Africa
**Position**: Defender
**Ht:** 6ft 1in
**Wt:** 12st 7lb
**Signed for Leeds:**
August 1994, for £275,000, from Mamelodi Sundowns
**Former clubs:**
Mamelodi Sundowns (SA)
1994 Leeds United
**Leeds record:**
53 apps, 10 goals

**Phil Masinga: not enough appearances to keep him in the country**

## *Robert* **Molenaar**

Robert Molenaar's Leeds career was much happier. Signed for £1 million from Dutch club Volendam, the six-foot three-inch central defender made his League debut in the 3–0 win over Leicester on 11 January 1997, having trained with his new team-mates for the first time only the day before.

**Robert MOLENAAR**

**Born:** 27 February 1969
**Birthplace:** Zaandam, Holland
**Position**: Defender
**Ht:** 6ft 2in
**Wt:** 14st 4lb
**Signed for Leeds:**
£1 million from Volendam (Hol)
**Former clubs:**
Volendam (Hol)

**Lucas Radebe: goalkeeper-turned-defender**

## *Lucas* **Radebe**

Regarded as the best player to emerge from South Africa, but beset by the same problems at Leeds as Phil Masinga, defender Radebe is a fine all-rounder who actually started as a goalkeeper and represented Bophuthatswana in the 1990 Homeland Games in that position.

**Lucas RADEBE**

**Born:** 12 April 1969
**Birthplace:** Johannesburg, South Africa
**Position**: Defender
**Ht:** 6ft 1in
**Wt:** 11st 9lb
**Signed for Leeds:**
5 September 1994, for £250,000, from Kaiser Chiefs
**Former clubs:**
Kaiser Chiefs (SA)
Leeds United
**Leeds record:**
19 apps, 6 goals

## *Bruno* **Ribeiro**

Star of Portugal's Under-21 side, left-sided midfielder Bruno Ribeiro was signed for £500,000 from Vitoria Setubal in the summer of 1997. Though he spoke no English, hopes are high that he will settle in quickly.

**Bruno RIBEIRO**

**Born: 22** October 1975
**Birthplace:** Setubal,Portugal
**Position**: Midfielder
**Ht:** 5ft 7in
**Wt:** 12st 7lb
**Signed for Leeds:**
June 1997, for £500,000, from Vitoria Setubal
**Former clubs:**
Vitoria Setubal (Por)
**Leeds record:**
0 apps, 0 goals

## *Frank* **Strandli**

Norwegian international Frank Strandli was, like Masinga, a expensive forward failure. He cost £350,000 when he arrived from IK Start in January 1993, but was sold to fellow-Norsemen Brann Bergen in November 1994 for £100,000 after just a handful of Premiership starts. Colombian hitman

**Frank STRANDLI**

**Born:** 16 May 1972
**Birthplace:** Norway
**Position**: Forward
**Ht:** 5ft 10in
**Wt:** 12st 7lb
**Signed for Leeds:**
January 1993, for £350,000, from IK Start
**Former clubs:**
IK Start (Nor)
1993 Leeds United
1994 Brann Bergen (Nor)
**Leeds record:**
14 apps,2 goals

**Summer 1997 signing Bruno Ribeiro clashes with Arsenal's David Platt**

Faustino Asprilla is another one who got away. In August 1995 he rejected Borussia Dortmund and was said to be "genuinely excited at the thought of linking up with Tony Yeboah at Leeds". But as we know, the temperamental entertainer joined Newcastle United instead.

# *Tony* Yeboah

When it comes to crowd-pleasers, Tony Yeboah ranks with the best. It seemed the search for a replacement for Lee Chapman had ended when Anthony Yeboah arrived at the ground, accompanied by Eintracht Frankfurt general manager Bernd Holzenbein, at lunchtime on Thursday 6 January 1995. The Ghanaian international was fed-up in Germany and anxious to explore new fields, providing the price was right. He was said to be seeking a salary in excess of £10,000 a week.

Howard Wilkinson and Bill Fotherby, the club's managing director, concluded a £3.4 million deal for the Bundesliga's joint leading scorer. Yeboah had scored 18 goals in 22 games for Eintracht Frankfurt in the 1993–94 season before being sidelined by injury. Wilko was keen to close the deal as he knew that Arsenal, Aston Villa and Newcastle United had all expressed an interest in the powerful striker.

"I came across Tony in Germany when he first played for Frankfurt", explained Wilkinson. "At that time the satellite TV programme *Football for Professionals* was on every Friday night. Yeboah had joined Frankfurt from a second-division club and was an overnight sensation...He just took the Bundesliga by storm and I would sit there week after week thinking to myself, 'Bloody hell, what a player he is.'

"Then he disappeared from view. I don't know whether it was because Eurosport stopped screening it or what, but he sort of faded from the front of my mind. Then I got a telephone call, followed by a fax, and the name on the fax leapt off the paper at me. Tony had been out injured and had got lost for 15 months, but was now available. Basically that was that. I went and signed him."

By 19 January 1995 Yeboah, armed with a work permit clearance, was ready to take the stage in English football. His future with Leeds had hung in the balance after the Professional Footballers' Association expressed its concern to the Department of Employment about a clause inserted in his contract enabling him to leave Elland Road after 12 months should he fail to settle in England.

The Ghanaian made his debut as a substitute in a 4–0 defeat of Queens Park Rangers on 24 January, and after another bit-part in a 1–1 draw at Blackburn made a scoring full debut in a 1–0 victory over Everton at Elland Road.

**Tony Yeboah: Wilkinson spotted him on German satellite television and made him a star at Leeds**

There was nothing languid about this man's grace. Cast in a different metal to Cantona, there is something heroic about his sheer power and commitment; and when he surges forward to within shooting range – which in his case can be anywhere from 40 yards or so – he rouses such hopeful anticipation in the onlooker that even some opposing fans are disappointed when he doesn't deliver a sensational finish.

In those opening games, wearing the Number Nine shirt, Tony blasted two goals against Chelsea, another pair against Leicester City, one past Coventry, a hat-trick against Ipswich, one at Newcastle United and another two in the Crystal Palace net – 12 goals in 16 (2) Premiership appearances. He was undoing England's best defences in the same relentless way he had destroyed the best in Germany.

Here for sure was a super talent, a special breed, a man apart who, through sheer strength of character and body, could mesmerise opponents, thrilling the gallery like the gladiators of Rome. When I first asked Howard Wilkinson to sum up this powerful goal machine he laughed: "He's an animal. A bit like a good ballet dancer, combining grace and ease with formidable strength".

The natural ability is there for all to see but it was no yellow-brick road Yeboah travelled to the land of gravy. Born and raised with seven brothers and sisters under the corrugated-iron roof of a two-room shack in the Ghanaian township of New Tafo, his prospects were strictly limited. The family had no running water and six families shared one toilet: yet despite the squalor and the obvious hardships Tony had one love to stimulate his lust for life – football.

From the time he learned to walk, Tony kicked anything and everything: tin cans, leaves bound together with string, makeshift balls of all shapes and sizes. Morning, noon and night, between school hours, he practised barefoot. Love turned to obsession; ambition became dedication.

Dreams are not easily fulfilled, and at 16 Tony went to work as a motor mechanic. He hated it, and could not wait to get home, peel off the oily overalls and practice with a ball. Eventually he persuaded his father, Mike, that his destiny was not in internal combustion but in explosive goalscoring!

Mike later revealed that having gone to watch his son play, "I was amazed how good he was competitively. At that moment I realised he had been given a gift from God and it was his duty to use it".

He played for local side Osa before joining the Kumasi Corner Stones and then the Okwawu team in Accra, where he was spotted by Saarbrücken, a German second-division outfit who eventually sold him to Frankfurt.

"Nothing he has done has surprised me because I knew what he could do", revealed Howard Wilkinson shortly before the 1996 Coca-Cola Cup Final. "I kept asking him what had happened to his whizz-bangs that he was scoring from everywhere in Germany. Headers, tap-ins, and every now and then he would walk on to one from 30 yards, or he would run with the ball, then – wallop! We are talking Bobby Charlton things here. Then he started to do it for us. I think it was confidence, really.

"When you see him score a goal like the ones he netted against Wimbledon or Liverpool, it all looks so easy. It is as if you are watching a ballerina, not a man."

The one at Wimbledon was part of a treble and was a blistering effort only bettered by the match-winning volley that ripped the heart out of Liverpool and earned Tony the Goal of the Year award. Add to that a spectacular hat-trick in Monte Carlo against Monaco, and the 1993 African Footballer of the Year was everything they said he was. But football is a fickle game. The goals dried up, the magic waned, as international calls and injuries impeded his progress at club level. A bust-up with new boss George Graham hit the headlines in December 1996. Yeboah revealed he was desperately unhappy and claimed he had been snubbed by Graham, who would not play him. He declared he was fit, the manager felt he was not.

Training, it is true, is not Yeboah's favourite activity, so when he failed to report on the first day of pre-season work for the 1997–98 campaign there were not too many raised eyebrows. Graham had indicated he wanted to make peace with his wayward star, whose agent Drew Tiffany claimed Yeboah was going against the advice he had been given. "We have told him he should come back as soon as possible and sort it out face-to-face", Tiffany explained.

**Tony YEBOAH**

**Born:** 6 June 1966
**Birthplace:** New Tafo, Ghana
**Position**: Forward
**Ht:** 5ft 10in
**Wt:** 13st 11lb
**Signed for Leeds:**
5 January 1995,
for £3.4 million, from Eintracht Frankfurt
**Former clubs:**
Osa (Gha)
Kumasi Corner Stones (Gha)
Okwawu (Gha)
Saarbrücken (Ger)
Eintracht Frankfurt (Ger)
Leeds United
**Leeds record:**
66 apps, 32 goals
**Honours:**
25 Ghanaian caps

# Chapter 8
# The Leeds Youth Policy

**Home-produced players are the lifeblood of most provincial clubs and Leeds' FA Youth Cup success in 1993 and 1997 emphasizes the club's commitment to youth.**

Young players have figured prominently in United's development since way back in the late 1920s when Dick Ray, a former Leeds City captain and committee-man, took over the managerial reins from Arthur Fairclough.

Fairclough had invested in star talent after winning promotion in 1924, introducing players such as Willis Edwards, Tom Jennings, Tom Townsley, Bobby Turnbull and Russell Wainscoat without success. Ray, a former full-back and Fairclough's one time assistant, took over in the summer of 1927.

Ray was an outspoken gentleman who liked to do things his way, and his policy of developing raw talent and honing it into top-class material proved very rewarding. The pick of the bunch to emerge under his careful guidance were George and Jimmy Milburn (cousins of Newcastle United legend "Wor Jackie"), Wilf Copping, Bert Sproston, Bill Furness, Eric Stephenson, Arthur Hydes and Tom Cochrane.

George Milburn was 18 when Ray snatched him from Ashington in March 1928. Then a centre-half, he was persuaded to play full-back and made the first of

**Jimmy (left) and George Milburn: two of three brothers – all fullbacks – who served United**

his 157 League appearances in this position the following November, in a home derby with Sheffield Wednesday. George and Jimmy, the youngest of the famous Leeds footballing family, were both ever-present full-backs in the season of 1932–33. Jimmy was only 16 when he arrived at Elland Road from Ashington, and his debut came in another derby game, a first-division fixture against Sheffield United in November 1939. As solid as a brick wall, Jimmy would have clocked up far more than his 208 League appearances for the club but for seven years of war, during which he was wounded fighting in Belgium in 1944.

Bert Sproston, who had been turned away by Huddersfield Town as a youngster, took over the right-back role from George at Chelsea just before Christmas 1934. Ray had found Bert as a 17-year-old playing with non-League Sandbach Ramblers and developed him into one of England's most cultured defenders. Capped eight times while with Leeds, it was only a mounting overdraft that forced the club to sell Bert to Tottenham Hotspur for a near-record £9,500 in June 1938, by which time he had made 130 League appearances.

Wilf Copping made his name with Arsenal following a £6,000 transfer to Highbury. A year earlier the "Iron Man", who at 5ft 7in was a pocket-battleship forerunner of Norman Hunter, had tackled his way into the England team. Barnsley-born Wilf was 20 when signed by Leeds from Middlecliffe Rovers in March 1929, and became the hard man in the famous Edwards-Hart-Copping half-back line, all of them England internationals.

Another shrewd deal by Dick Ray was the £50 he laid out to take 19-year-old Billy Furness from Usworth Colliery in 1928. Blooded in the Division One game with Middlesbrough in November 1929, the inside-left matured into another full England international during his nine years at Elland Road; and when he did leave for Norwich City, United pocketed a handsome fee of £2,700. Yet another of Ray's protegés to be capped by England was Eric Stephenson. Given his chance against Portsmouth, he was an outstanding inside-left but, alas, was killed on active service in Burma in 1944, as a Major in the Ghurka Rifles.

A scoring debut at 19 by Arthur Hydes, against Blackburn Rovers in January 1931, set the spikey-haired centre-forward on his way. The former toffee-factory worker, signed from Ardsley Recreation in May 1930, made a right toffee-apple out of many of the top defenders of the time, netting 74 goals in 127 League outings.

Yes: Dick Ray could look back on a highly successful youth policy, which also included persuading 20-year-old left-winger Tom Cochrane to turn professional. Cochrane, though he struggled at first, made a major contribution to the 1931–32 promotion campaign and played in 244 League games, scoring 23 goals.

Ray's successor, Billy Hampson – who at the age of 41 years and eight months won an FA Cup-winners' medal with Newcastle United in 1924 – continued to develop the youth programme at Elland Road, and his crop of young hopefuls won the Central League championship for the first and only time in 1936–37. Unfortunately the outbreak of war prevented them enjoying their football maturity, and it was not until Major Frank Buckley (an ardent advocate of youth development) took charge for five years between 1948 and 1953 that United once again profited from the success of home-grown talent.

It was the Major who unearthed one of the game's most outstanding talents, and certainly United's greatest pre-Revie player: John Charles. The Welshman was signed on his 16th birthday and was playing international football for Wales at 18. A six-foot-one-and-a-half-inch man-mountain who was equally effective at centre-forward or centre-half, he made the first of his 308 League appearances (153 goals) at Blackburn Rovers at the age of 17 and, of course, was eventually sold to Juventus for a then-world record £65,000.

Another teenager to develop through the Buckley academy was Aubrey Powell, who had been spotted as an amateur with Swansea Town in 1935. The inside-forward made his first division debut in a 5–0 victory over Middlesbrough on Christmas Day 1936 aged 18, and went on to play for Wales despite being written off by the doctors the following year after breaking a leg at Preston. He was eventually sold in 1948, along with Irish international Con Martin, to wipe out a crippling overdraft.

## *Revie revives youth scheme*

It was left to Don Revie to revive the club's flagging youth scheme when he took charge in 1961. A man of immense patience and foresight, he knew both the club's future and his own lay in the development of a successful youth policy, and left nothing to chance. Organising the whole scheme from beginning to end with meticulous professionalism, Revie orchestrated a scouting system second to none. Young players arriving at Leeds were treated with respect, and indoctrinated with the elements of professional football that would one day make them among the best in Europe.

Revie spent 13 years at the helm, during which time he moulded some of the game's great names. Billy Bremner, it is true, was given his senior debut at Chelsea in January 1960 by Jack Taylor, but it was Revie who nurtured the young Scot and ironed out the creases that often rubbed authority up the wrong way.

From the Revie stable emerged waves of exciting talent. Goalkeeper Gary Sprake; the ever-reliable Paul Reaney; Terry Cooper, who made a surprise debut on the day Leeds gained promotion to Division One in 1964 as a left-winger but later consolidated his position as an England full-back; Norman "Never-Let-You-Down" Hunter, who bred fear in the hearts of all opponents; Terry Yorath, a ball-winning midfielder; master of the dribble Eddie Gray; Paul Madeley, who could fit in anywhere at any level; Mick Bates, who covered for Bremner and Giles in midfield; Rod Belfitt, a constructive forward who served an apprenticeship as a draughtsman before joining Leeds at 18 from Retford Town; Terry Hibbitt, signed from school, who made a sensational debut against Nottingham Forest in February 1966, when after being thrown on as a substitute he scored with his first touch.

Then there was goalkeeper David Harvey, another local lad who worked in a shoe factory before joining United, and later became a Scottish international; Leeds' youngest debutant, Peter Lorimer, the hot-shot who smashed in more than 200 goals after making his debut against Southampton aged just 15 years and 289 days; and Frank Gray, who, though not as gifted as his older brother Eddie, still won 32 caps for Scotland.

United have continued to enjoy the fruits of their investment in home-grown talent. Since the Revie era, the club has had nine managers. Some have not stayed long enough to make any impression but others, such as Gray, Bremner, Howard Wilkinson and now George Graham, have never been shy to give youth its fling.

Just look at some of the great players who have rolled off the United assembly-line in recent years. David Batty, the tigerish midfield ball-winner honed in the shadow of Bremner and now starring with Newcastle United and England; John Lukic, who kept David Seaman out of goal; winger Scott Sellars, who went on to play for Blackburn Rovers and Newcastle; "Big Jon" Newsome, the centre-half sold to Norwich City for £1 million; and Gary Speed, the exciting striker now knocking them in for Everton.

One man who has experienced it from all angles is Eddie Gray, now youth team coach. Brought to Elland Road from Glasgow as a youngster by United's then-chief scout John Barr, Eddie become a household name as a player and later manager between 1982 and '85 and received the MBE for services to football.

What does Eddie look for when assessing a young player? "First of all, you look for natural ability. If he has a good attitude, is he a fit lad? If he satisfies these points you have something to work on."

The ability to nurture young talent earned Leeds FA Youth Cup victories in 1993 and 1997, and a glance at the current senior squad shows just how successful United are at raising their own. "It's a big step up to the first team", he says, "but a lot of these boys have the ability to cope with it. Sometimes it's the boys you don't think are going to do it who surprise you. They develop late. So we'll just have to wait and see."

**Versatile England Under-21 player Andy Couzens**

# *Lee* **Matthew**

Middlesbrough-born midfielder Lee was the hero of the 1997 FA Youth Cup Final second leg when he scored the decisive goal against Crystal Palace in the second half at Selhurst Park.

# *Wes* **Boyle**
# *Matthew* **Jones**

Also members of the 1997 FA Youth Cup-winning side, Wes and Matthew bagged Leeds' two goals in the first leg of the final.

# *Andy* **Couzens**

Defender Andy Couzens is an adaptable performer who can operate almost anywhere. An England Under-21, he was blooded in the League against Coventry City in March 1995 and replaced John Pemberton during the UEFA Cup tie against Monaco.

# *Mark* **Jackson**

Barnsley-born central defender Mark Jackson's debut came as a substitute against Middlesbrough in March 1996. He madehis first start against Leicester City that September, dropped out of the side but quickly returned. An England Under-18 cap, he only turned 20 on 30 September 1997.

# *Nicky* **Byrne**

Goalkeeper Nicky Byrne was only 16 when he was included in the first-team squad at Southampton in August 1995. He was cover for John Lukic, who played, but was called up because second choice Mark Beeney was suspended for one match after being sent off in a reserve game and third choice Paul Pettinger was on loan to Rotherham.

**England Under-21 international Mark Ford led Leeds to victory in the FA Youth Cup**

# *Mark* **Ford**

Midfielder Mark Ford, also an England Under-21 international, is seen as another David Batty in the making. Hard and competitive, he is a tigerish tackler whose commitment earned him more than 20 starts in the 1995–96 season. The captain of United's victorious 1992–93 FA Youth Cup team, Mark made his senior debut against Swindon in the final game of the 1993–94 season.

# *Mark* **Tinkler**

A broken ankle sustained during the 1993–94 season somewhat hampered Mark Tinkler's progress, but he came back in impressive style in 1996–97.

**Mark Tinkler: bad break**

The midfield general has already added to his silverware, having helped England win the European Under-18 Youth Championship. Mark's senior debut came in the derby clash with Sheffield United in April 1993, and he remained on the fringe of the first team until suffering an unfortunate injury during a reserve-team match. He was given an extra incentive when he played against Monaco in the UEFA Cup in 1995, and made it into the senior side for 1996–97.

**1993, and United's cubs celebrate after clinching the FA Youth Cup. Four years later they did it again**

## *Rob* **Bowman**

Rob Bowman was a graduate of Durham junior football and was only 17 when he made a glamorous entry on to the senior stage against Manchester United. He struggled to establish himself at this level, and in February 1997 left Leeds on a free transfer to join Rotherham United.

## *Harry* **Kewell**

19-year-old Harry Kewell is a young Australian from Sydney who is progressing well. A product of the New South Wales Soccer Academy, he graduated through the youth and reserve ranks at Elland Road, winning a first-team appearance as a substitute against Middlesbrough in March 1996. Essentially a midfield player, he then played left-back in the 1–0 victory over Southampton. Though he fancies the left side. Harry can operate virtually anywhere – full-back, centre-back, midfield or centre-forward.

## *Gary* **Kelly**

Gary Kelly, who arrived from Dublin club Home Farm as a pacy, two-footed 17-year-old winger is, at the age of 23, a seasoned international star with close on 200 senior appearances to his name. Gary had made only three substitute appearances – his first, in a League Cup tie against Scunthorpe United, coming within a month of his arrival – before the start of the 1993–94 season. Then Howard Wilkinson pushed him to wing-back and his career took off. Within a year he was first-choice right-back for Jack Charlton's Republic of Ireland World Cup squad, and participated in the 1994 finals in the USA.

# Ian **Harte**

Keeping it in the family is Gary's nephew Ian Harte from Drogheda, also a promising right-back who has played in the same senior eleven with Gary, who switched to the left. Ian, also a full Republic of Ireland international, graduated to the United team as a substitute against Reading in the Coca-Cola Cup.

# Stephen **McPhail**

Hailing from the Republic of Ireland, left-sided midfielder Stephen was a key member of the 1997 FA Youth Cup side and shows a lot of natural ability.

# Alan **Maybury**

Another young Irish player and Youth Cup veteran, right-back Alan has proved to be very quick both in defence and when going forward.

# Jamie **Forrester**

Jamie Forrester was billed as United's "secret weapon" when he blasted Crewe Alexandra out of the FA Cup in January 1994. The former FA School of Excellence pupil was 19 years old, and a surprise choice for the third-round tie.

The irony was that Crewe boss Dario Gradi was somewhat relieved when he scanned the team sheet and realised rookie Forrester was partnering Brian Deane in attack. He said later: "We were afraid David White would play, and I didn't think our defender Gus Wilson could have coped with White's pace and aerial ability. I really thought Forrester was tailor-made for him".

It just shows even the experts get it wrong sometimes: for Jamie took Crewe apart. Wilkinson had rescued the Bradford-born teenager from French club Auxerre, but after six games in the 1992–93 season his progress was interrupted by a hernia operation. The return to the first team against Crewe proved the capabilities of the youngster who first made his mark with a spectacular overhead-kick goal in the 1993 FA Youth Cup Final against Manchester United.

Since leaving Leeds, Jamie has made his mark in the lower divisions, making 50 League appearances for Grimsby and 10 for Scunthorpe.

# Jason **Blunt**

Jason Blunt first appeared in the youth team in 1992–93, but made the headlines in October 1995 when Eric Cantona was injured in his comeback reserve game following a challenge from the Leeds youngster. Jason was eventually given his chance by Howard Wilkinson following the Coca-Cola Cup Final shambles in March 1996, and after a substitute appearance against Middlesbrough made his full debut at home to Southampton.

**Jamie Forrester: fondly remembered for taking Crewe to the cleaners in the 1993–94 FA Cup**

# Chapter 9

# The Great Matches

**Leeds United have featured in well over 3,000 competitive matches since entering the second division of the Football League in 1920 and have played in countless memorable matches – far too many, of course, to be recorded here. But the following selection, while not all classic encounters, have been significant in some way or other in forging the club's history.**

## *The first game*

Leeds United were born out of the ashes of the defunct and disgraced Leeds City and took the field on 28 August 1920 for their first match, in the Football League second division against Port Vale – the team which had taken over City's fixtures a year earlier!

United had started with nothing just a few months earlier, so it was hardly surprising that most of the players lacked Football League experience. Nevertheless, the team gave a very good account of itself and only went down to a 2–0 defeat in the second half.

**28 AUGUST 1920**

**Football League**
**Division Two**
Recreation Ground, Hanley

**Port Vale (0) 2**
**Leeds United (0) 0**
HT: 0–0

**Team:**
Down, Duffield, Tillotson, Musgrove, Baker, Walton, Mason, Goldthorpe, Thompson, Lyons, Best

United enjoyed the better of the exchanges in the first half, but the forwards just could not make the breakthrough, although former Bradford City inside-right Ernie Goldthorpe had an excellent game as did another of the more experienced players, ex-Huddersfield centre-half Jim Baker.

In the end, Vale's experience told and they scored twice in the second half to win the game. Two weeks later, however, Leeds won their first game and this time Vale were the victims, going down 3–1 at Elland Road. Scorers were Matt Ellson, signed from Frickley Colliery, with two, and one from Jerry Best.

## *A record score*

Leeds overwhelmed FA Cup semi-finalists Leicester City to set up a club record League victory of 8–0.

As is often the case, United did not start well and could have been two goals down in the opening 15 minutes. The Milburn brothers at the back seemed

**Dubliner Harry Duggan scored 45 goals in 187 League appearances and led the rout of Leicester City**

**7 APRIL 1934**

**Football League Division One**
Elland Road

**Leeds United (4) 8**
(Duggan 2, Mahon 2, Furness 2, Firth 2)
**Leicester City (0) 0**

**Team:**
Moore; Milburn G, Milburn J; Edwards, Hart, Copping; Mahon, Firth, Duggan, Furness, Cochrane

troubled by the swirling wind, and 'keeper Moore had to find his best form to save good attempts from Liddle and Maw.

The half-back line, strengthened by the return of Willis Edwards after a three-month absence, began to dominate and Leicester had difficulty getting out of their own half. McLaren, in goal, had a thankless task as Mahon peppered him with crosses; and it was from one of his dashing raids that Duggan converted the first goal. Mahon then added a second and fourth himself before half-time, the third having been notched by Furness.

Leicester gallantly tried to raise their game but there was no stopping this rampant Leeds side. Furness, Duggan and Firth (2) added four more to complete a phenomenal whitewash.

**Goals timetable:**
25 Duggan *(cross-shot).* 33 Mahon *(low shot).*
35 Furness *(close-range shot).* 44 Mahon *(strong shot).*
48 Furness *(from 12 yards).* 60 Duggan *(angled shot).*
62 Firth *(close range).*
78 Firth *(tapped in Mahon's pass).*

# *Leicester hit for eight again*

Leeds, not known as a free-scoring side, seem to save their bullets for Leicester, for yet again the Midlanders conceded eight goals, perhaps as a result of an injury to 'keeper Mclaren in the 30th minute: his studs stuck in the mud as he tried to turn sharply and he tore the tendons of an instep. Deputizing, Sharman was beaten within a minute of donning the jersey, and Frame in his turn between the posts could do nothing to contain the blistering onslaught.

The *Yorkshire Post* reported: "It is a matter of speculation how many of the shots which scored would have been stopped by an experienced goalkeeper; but to the onlooker it seemed that the majority would have beaten anyone."

**1 OCTOBER 1938**

**Football League Division One**
Elland Road

**Leeds United (3) 8**
(Hodgson 5, Hargreaves, Milburn, Cochrane)

**Leicester City (0) 2**
(Baines, Bowers)

**Team:**
Twomey; Milburn, Gadsby, Makinson, Holley, Brown; Cochrane, Thomson, Hodgson, Powell, Hargreaves

Leeds played two reserve wingers, Cochrane and Hargreaves, the former putting on a dazzling show, controlling the ball with either foot and "displaying any amount of elusive trickery". The only regular forward available, Hodgson, claimed five goals. It seemed there was no stopping him once he had smelt blood with the opening strike.

**Goals timetable:**
32 Hodgson *(header from Makinson cross).*
37 Hodgson *(shot from Cochrane's centre).*
43 Hodgson *(shot from Hargreaves' pass).*
57 Hargreaves *(first-time shot from Cochrane cross).*
59 Baines, Leicester *(header).*
64 Milburn *(penalty: Reeday fouled Cochrane).*
72 Hodgson *(shot from acute angle).*
73 Hodgson *(shot from Cochrane's pass).*
82 Cochrane *(shot on the run).*
87 Bowers, Leicester *(shot).*

# *No, no, no, Ref!*

Leeds were floored by a moment of controversy when Boston referee Ray Tinkler allowed a goal which even embarrassed West Brom's Tony Brown, leading to a home defeat for Don Revie's championship-chasing side at a time when they needed every point. It cost them a goal, it cost them the game, it nearly provoked a riot, and the repercussions were far more severe – for it probably cost them the League title too.

The drama exploded in the 70th minute. Albion, prompted by the sprightly Asa Hartford, had been the more fluent and positive side but were clinging on desperately to a lead created in the 18th minute, when Tony Brown took advantage of a hesitant defence to score. Then Hunter tried a pass that really wasn't on. The ball struck Brown, who was just inside his own area, on the legs and ricocheted over the half-way line into Leeds' territory where Suggett stood all alone.

That he was in an offside position there is no doubt: but

**Billy Bremner leads the vocal barrage of referee Ray Tinkler during that infamous defeat by West Brom**

as Brown gave chase, Suggett cleverly drifted away. Brown hesitated, realizing Suggett's situation and seeing that the linesman, W. Troupe of South Shields, had his flag raised. But the referee ignored the signal and Brown motored on.

He was first to the ball and ran with it towards Sprake's goal before passing to Astle, who also appeared to be offside. It was a gift goal for the England centre-forward: 0–2. United were dead. "Nine months' hard work gone down the drain by a referee's decision," was how Revie bitterly summed it all up.

Company secretary Tinkler's after-match explanation was: "As far as I am concerned the player (Suggett) was not interfering with play, the player with the ball was not offside and therefore there was no need to whistle. That was what I asked the linesman and he agreed." Few at Elland Road, or the thousands watching on TV that night, would agree that Suggett was not interfering with play: his part was crucial to the break.

It took five minutes or so to clear the pitch of angry fans, who had already voiced their disapproval when, just after the break, Jones had a seemingly-good goal disallowed for offside. Clarke did slot a neatly-taken goal in, but it came too late to make any difference.

**17 APRIL 1971**

**Football League Division One**
Elland Road

**Leeds United (0) 1**
(Clarke 85)

**W.B.A. (1) 2**
(Brown 18, Astle 70)

**Team:**
Sprake; Reaney, Cooper; Bremner, Charlton, Hunter; Bates (Davey), Clarke, Jones, Giles, Gray

# *Kop left speechless*

A stirring two-goal victory at Anfield endorsed the claim that Leeds United were one of the game's major powers. The way they ended Liverpool's unbeaten run of 35 League games at Anfield was so decisive the Kop was left speechless.

Barry Foster in the *Yorkshire Post* wrote: "Leeds' all-round efficiency was so great that Charlton, who has been the cornerstone of a defence that has been beaten only once in nearly two months, was not missed."

Sprake, despite an injured back, was in spectacular form, particularly in the first half when Liverpool enjoyed their best spell: and though this was a brilliant team effort, with each man playing his part, Clarke and Giles were also worthy of special praise.

Clarke, whose penetrating runs made him a night-

**1 JANUARY, 1972**

**Football League Division One**
Anfield

**Liverpool (0) 0**
(Brown 18, Astle 70)

**Leeds United (0) 2**
(Clarke 60, Jones 81)

**Team:**
Sprake; Reaney, Cooper; Bremner, Madeley, Hunter; Lorimer, Clarke, Jones, Giles, Gray (Bates)

mare to mark, scored the first goal with a well-directed header on the hour. It stemmed from a Giles free kick straight on to the head of Madeley, who turned the ball square for Clarke to run on to. Clemence was beaten again 21 minutes later. Clarke sped down the right, cleverly holding the ball until Jones had a clear run at goal. Releasing his pass precisely, he slipped the ball into Jones's path and the burly striker crashed his shot home from the edge of the box as Clemence, Ross and Callaghan challenged. This victory put Leeds second in Division One.

# *Table-toppers*

David Batty had good reason to celebrate as his well-struck shot flew past goalkeeper Steve Cherry into the Notts County net. It helped Leeds secure their first home win in two months and set up a convincing 3–0 victory which put them back on top of Division One.

All this was achieved without centre-forward Lee Chapman who was nursing a broken wrist. Strachan, Batty and Steve Hodge, who had been given his chance because of "Chappy's" injury, were the driving force behind this victory.

**1 FEBRUARY 1992**

**Football League Division One**
Elland Road

**Leeds United (1) 3**
(Sterland 12, Batty 57, Wallace 77)

**Notts County (0) 0**

**Team:**
Lukic; Sterland, Fairclough, Whyte, Dorigo; Strachan, Batty, McAllister, Hodge; Speed, Wallace

County were vulnerable on crosses, and with 'keeper Cherry crippled by injury it was no surprise when Leeds cashed in. Mel Sterland had given them a lead in the 12th minute following indecision at the back, and County's defence was all at sea again in the 77th minute when Rod Wallace, who had run them ragged all afternoon, headed the third.

# *A third championship*

Leeds had set the pace at the top of the League for a long time, but the feeling was that it was Manchester United's title to lose. Having already knocked Leeds out of both the League and FA Cups, the Red Devils had games in hand and were looking good – until

**Jon Newsome gets in on the scoring act at Bramall Lane**

**26 APRIL 1992**

**Football League Division 1**
Bramall Lane, Sheffield

**Sheffield United (1) 2**
(Cork, Chapman o.g.)
**Leeds United (1) 3**
(Wallace, Newsome, Gayle o.g.)

**Team:**
Lukic, Newsome, Dorigo, Batty, Fairclough, Whyte, Strachan (Cantona), Wallace, Chapman, McAllister (Hodge), Speed

**An exultant Rod Wallace (right) and Eric Cantona celebrate the decisive own goal by Sheffield United's Brian Gayle which set the seal on Leeds' resounding 3–2 victory at Bramall Lane**

**Eric Cantona hits United's fourth goal in the FA Charity Shield triumph at Wembley**

mid-April, when things suddenly went off the rails.

Leeds' 41st match was set for lunchtime on Sunday 8 May, away to Sheffield United. Manchester's 41st match was due to kick off three hours later, and it was a much tougher proposition: against Liverpool at Anfield. With a two-point advantage Leeds could claim the title if they and Liverpool both won.

But Yorkshire derbies are no place for the faint-hearted and any team coached by Dave Bassett would never stop trying, even if their play wouldn't attract purrs of satisfaction from the purists. The Blades took the lead with a simple goal from veteran Alan Cork after 28 minutes, but Leeds equalized just before the break with the first of three freakish goals. Gordon Strachan took a quick free kick into the penalty area, Brian Gayle attempted to clear it but it bounced off Gary Speed, then Rod Wallace, to end up in the net.

Jon Newsome scored Leeds' second goal after 65 minutes, with a deft stooping header. Although two more goals were to follow, Newsome's was to be the last one scored in the right end. Two minutes after taking the lead, Lee Chapman turned John Pemberton's shot over the goal-line. Unfortunately for Leeds, the players were not team-mates yet, and that made the score 2–2.

After 77 minutes, the game was decided. Gayle, who had already aided Leeds' cause with his hashed clearance for their first goal, found himself in a race with Eric Cantona and Rod Wallace to deal with the danger caused by an errant pass from Sheffield's David Barnes. Gayle won the race, but his header looped over goalkeeper Mel Rees and bounced into the net.

The title returned to Elland Road just over three hours later when Liverpool beat Manchester United 2–0.

## *Charity Shield magic*

The honour of appearing in the first-ever game of the Premier League era fell, appropriately enough, to two of the great teams of the Football League of the 1960s and '70s. Leeds United, as the final champions of the four-division Football League, met Liverpool, FA Cup-winners over Sunderland, at Wembley on a baking hot Saturday 8 August 1993 to contest the annual curtain-raiser to the new season, the FA Charity Shield.

Working on the premise that if something isn't broken, don't fix it, United boss Howard Wilkinson named exactly the same 11 players to start this game as had started the final match of the League Championship-clinching season three months earlier. This meant there was no place in the starting line-up for either £2 million summer signing David Rocastle – who would fail to fit in at Elland Road – or for inspirational midfielder Gordon Strachan, who had undergone back surgery in the offseason.

However, there was the talismanic, enigmatic genius of Frenchman Eric Cantona and he absolutely stole the show. The tackles may not have had the intensity of a Premier League battle, but the will to win was just as strong and Cantona displayed his relish for the big stage by netting a breathtaking hat-trick, including one magical run and shot past bemused Liverpool debutant keeper David James. Tony Dorigo got United's other goal, but a worrying trend was immediately noticeable because the Leeds defence was not at its water-tight best, conceding three goals.

Still, it was United fans who went away happier into the new season on the back of their 4–3 victory.

**8 AUGUST 1992**

**FA Charity Shield**
Wembley

**Leeds United (2) 4**
(Cantona 3, Dorigo)
**Liverpool (1) 3**

**Team:**
Lukic, Newsome (Hodge), Dorigo, Batty, Fairclough, Whyte, Cantona, Wallace, Chapman (Strachan), McAllister, Speed

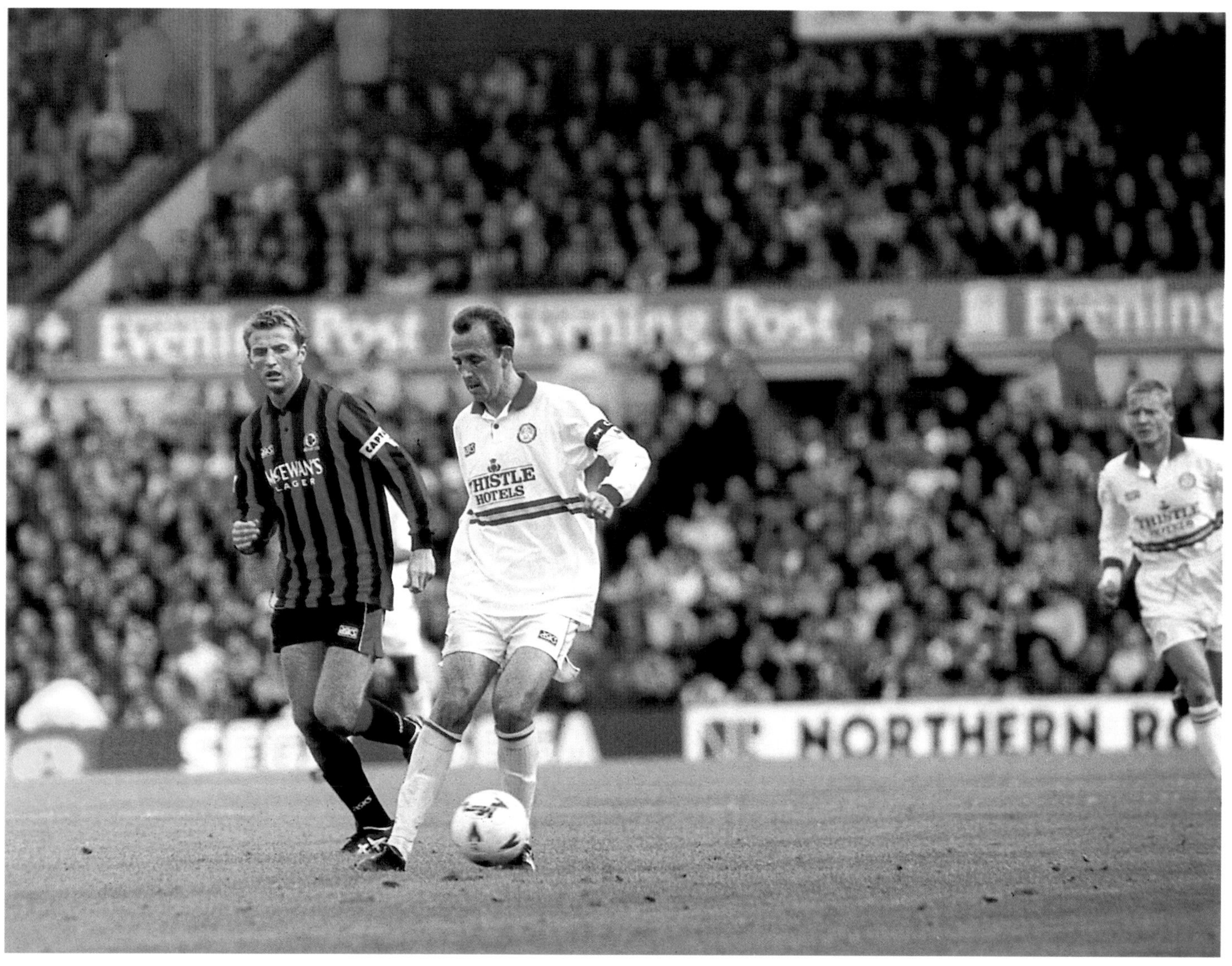


**Alan Shearer fires Blackburn ahead: he would beat Mark Beeney twice more in a 3–3 thriller**

# *Six-goal thriller*

This was a classic that kept the fans on their toes. Blackburn arrived at Elland Road unbeaten away from home, Leeds were unbeaten anywhere for six games and, what is more, both teams still had an interest in the championship.

In the early minutes David Rocastle found himself inside the six-yard box with a clear chance, but Rovers goalkeeper Bobby Mimms dived to his left to save.

He was nowhere near a rasping effort from Brian Deane which smashed on to a post, but then denied the striker with a smothering save. At this stage Leeds were making all the running when, out of the blue, Rovers scored.

Alan Shearer, who had hardly had a touch in 20 minutes, tapped the ball over the line after Mark Beeney had palmed away Mike Newell's header.

Shearer made it 2–0 a minute into the second half. Once again Stuart Ripley had engineered the opening with a speedy run to give the England centre-forward another tap-in from two yards.

A rousing cheer greeted the introduction of substitute David Batty, but it was a rash challenge from behind by David May on Deane which opened the door. Gary McAllister made no mistake from the penalty spot.

A lack of concentration, however, cost Leeds dear. They seemed to be taken unawares when Newell knocked a quick free-kick to Shearer, who picked his spot to complete his hat-trick.

With eight minutes to go, Mimms conceded a corner from which Mark Newsome drilled home a powerful shot, with the help of a deflection, from eight yards.

Leeds had the buzz now and attacked ferociously. Mimms was unsettled and the pressure told, as McAllister's shot appeared to go in off the chest of Tim Sherwood.

**23 OCTOBER 1993**

**FA Carling Premiership**
Elland Road

**Leeds United (0) 3**
(McAllister 56 (pen), 86, Newsome 82)

**Blackburn Rovers (1) 3**
(Shearer 20, 46, 75)

**Team:**
Beeney; Kelly, Dorigo, Fairclough, Newsome, Wetherall (Batty), Rocastle (Whelan), McAllister, Speed, Wallace, Deane

# *100 and out*

**7 MAY 1994**

**FA Carling Premiership**
County Ground, Swindon

**Swindon Town (0) 0**
**Leeds United (2) 5**
(Deane 2, Fairclough, White, Wallace)

**Team:**
Lukic, Kelly, Pemberton, Fairclough, O'Leary, Wetherall, Strachan (Ford), Wallace, Deane, McAllister, White (Whelan)

Swindon Town had not enjoyed their 1993–94 season in the FA Carling Premiership. Without a victory until late November, their relegation back to the first division after one season in the top flight had long been confirmed.

However, they were determined to end the season on a high note with the visit of Leeds to the County Ground. For United there was definitely something to play for; a top-five finish, a huge improvement on the disappointing 17th as defending champions a year earlier.

Leeds got off to a great start with a couple of early goals and put the game out of reach for the Robins. But they had a big target to defend because with 95 goals conceded from the first 41 games, Swindon wanted to avoid the ignominy of becoming the first Premiership club to concede 100 goals.

Leeds, however, were in irresistible form and when the final whistle went on the final game of the season, Chris Fairclough, David White, Rod Wallace and Brian Deane, twice, had all found the target, without a single reply from Swindon.

# *Rush of goals*

There was no eight-goal celebration against Leicester City this time around, but it nonetheless proved a highly significant afternoon for George Graham.

Missing six regulars through injury, suspension and international call-ups, he introduced Robert Molenaar, a 27-year-old Dutch centre-half, who immediately looked worth his £1 million price-tag.

It had been a week of shocks. Kevin Keegan had resigned up at Newcastle and United's veteran striker Ian Rush, enduring the worst goal drought of his career – just one goal in 22 games – had told the gaffer he would not be offended if he was replaced by a

**It's in at last! Ian Rush shoots for his first goal against newly-promoted Leicester City**

**11 JANUARY 1997**

**FA Carling Premiership**
Elland Road

**Leeds United (2) 3**
(Bowyer, Rush 2)
**Leicester City (0) 0**

**Team:**
Martyn; Molenaar, Wetherall, Beesley, Kelly, Bowyer, Wallace, Jackson, Dorigo; Rush, Deane

**Lee Bowyer shows his delight after opening the scoring against Leicester City**

younger man. But Graham kept faith with the Liverpool legend and would be thankful he did.

Two goals from Rush, and one from Lee Bowyer, gave Leeds their first victory in seven games.

Not a vintage performance, but a badly-needed one to restore general morale and "Rushie"'s own confidence. It certainly gave hope that the man who made goalscoring an art was again going to write his name into the record books.

It was midfield dynamo Bowyer who broke the ice. Brian Deane was hardly troubled as he stood his ground to lay off a header from Tony Dorigo's deep cross, his knock-back making it easy for the young star in the 40th minute.

Five minutes later Bowyer paved the way for Rush to get in on the scoring act at last when he drilled in a crisp shot which was blocked on the line. As the ball hung in the air, the ace marksman arrived to poach a golden goal with a header from a yard out.

This put Leeds comfortably in control and they should have added a stack of goals to their tally. But there was just one more – and it came from Rush. A mis-kick by Dorigo wrong-footed the Leicester defenders, who were again tricked by Deane's astute flick which set Rush up for a volley from eight yards.

# *A K-O for Boro*

It is true that Leeds were only the supporting cast in this final show-down of the 1996–97 season but the eyes of the world were focused on Elland Road as Middlesbrough, double cup finalists and sporting the magical skills of Juninho, Ravanelli and Emerson, fought for their Premiership lives. Nothing short of victory could save them from relegation.

The atmosphere was electric as the fans were treated to the most dramatic 90 minutes of the season. Bryan Robson's Boro were understandably the more nervous for they had everything to lose, but Leeds, obviously stimulated by the occasion, were determined to put on a show.

George Graham had concentrated on organising his defence, and since the turn of the year United had earned a reputation as one of the meanest sides in the Premiership and nil-nil specialists.

Goalkeeper Nigel Martyn, the best in England on this form, broke Teesside's hearts when in the 14th minute he showed just why Leeds gave nothing away. Phil Stamp looked certain to score but was thwarted by the big man.

Pulses raced as Mikkel Beck raced on to a brilliant through ball from Juninho in the 55th minute, but the Dane was not up to it. The tension of the Boro fans poured out: one could feel for them as their hopes were raised with every attack.

All that suddenly changed in the 76th minute. Rod Wallace lifted a teasing cross into the Boro goalmouth and Brian Deane rose at the far post to head firmly past goalkeeper Ben Roberts.

It looked like the end but Juninho, sweating blood, continued to probe and one last mighty effort carried him into the Leeds area. His shot was not as crisp as he would have wished but the ball clipped Bowyer's foot and looped beyond Martyn's reach … 1–1!

Boro tried desperately to win themselves some luck as the clock ticked through stoppage time but it wasn't to be. The final whistle also blew time on their stay in the Premiership.

**11 MAY 1997**

**FA Carling Premiership**
Elland Road

**Leeds United (0) 1**
(Deane)
**Middlesbrough (0) 1**
(Juninho)

**Team:**
Martyn; Kelly, Dorigo, Radebe, Wetherall, Sharpe, Rush (Wallace), Deane, Bowyer, Lilley, Halle

**Ian Rush is thwarted by Emerson during the emotional final battle with Middlesbrough**

# Chapter 10
# At Home

**Faced with ever-increasing costs, first-class football clubs have had to seek additional income by broadening their commercial horizons. Leeds has been quick to seize the opportunities on offer**

Professional football is big business these days, and as such must look to develop and invest in the future. Leeds United have, since the days of Revie, always been at the forefront of commercial activity; and as we roll towards the millennium, exciting new developments at Elland Road keep the club in tune with the 21st century.

United have linked up with progressive Leeds City Council in its efforts to improve the public amenities of this famous old city. The council wanted to build a multi-purpose indoor arena to stage concerts, exhibitions and sporting activities, such as ice hockey and basketball. The city has long needed such a facility, and when Caspian, owners of Leeds United, tendered for the work and were chosen as preferred bidder, the foundation-stone of an exciting new chapter in United's history was laid.

## Rebuilding Elland Road

The new complex will be an extension of the Elland Road ground, also involving the refurbishment of the West Stand. In Phase Two, the West Stand's roof will be taken off so another tier can be added. The roof will

**The cavernous new stand which helped make Elland Road a Euro '96 venue**

then be replaced and the new arena built on to the back of the West Stand. Work will begin in late 1997 and is due for completion in June 1999.

The additional tier for the West Stand will also increase Elland Road's capacity by a further 5,000, bringing match attendances up to a potential maximum of 45,000.

## More than a football club

United have already obtained the franchise for ice hockey in West Yorkshire and are now starting to look for the Billy Bremners and Norman Hunters of the sport to build a team which will play under the name of Leeds Lasers.

Says Club secretary Nigel Pleasants: "We are also obviously looking at basketball and staging exhibitions and so on. Chris Akers, the chairman of Caspian, sees it as the Madison Square Garden of Yorkshire – a venue fit to stage the biggest, most prestigious sporting and non-sporting events in the world."

The complex will be huge, seating between 10,500 and 13,000 people, depending on its configuration – a capacity greater than that of Wembley Stadium's Empire Pool.

**New signings like Jimmy Floyd Hasselbaink (l) and Alf Inge Haaland are investments in Leeds' future**

Says Nigel: "The Arena is an exciting project: the overall package will probably cost in the region of £35 million, including the refurbishment of the West Stand. Building actually starts from the other end – the Fullerton Car Park end – and eventually they will join it all up.

"This is the way football has to develop, without question. We have to be realistic and recognise that we will not sell to our full capacity at every football game, whether we are in the Premiership or not. A lot of games will be sell-outs, of course, but we have to look in other directions to sustain our income.

"One major plus with the Arena is that all the corporate facilities will be shared. If someone takes an executive box in the Arena, the plan is that they will also get 10 seats for the football, and vice versa. On a football day they will be able to use their box for hospitality, then wander through and watch the football.

"Likewise the executive box-holders in the football ground will be able to avail themselves of the same facilities for events in the Arena, such as ice hockey and basketball. The whole thing will be linked."

## Corporate identity

United, then, are playing to their strengths in the brave new world of corporate hospitality.

Finance is all-important, of course, and the current trend is for the major players in the Premiership to launch themselves on the stock market – seen as essential in providing the ability to raise money by using City institutions.

You will not find Leeds United quoted here, however; they have tackled the issue in a different way, for they are already listed under the Caspian Group banner. Caspian own the club, having bought 94 per cent of Leeds United's holdings. The new owners quickly made their presence felt by investing more than £30 million, swallowing up the shares of the previous directors and investing money in team-building.

The Arena project includes an option for the club to buy back the Elland Road stadium from the council. With the freehold back in club hands, United will have more clout when dealing with the City. As Nigel Pleasants says: "This is very important. If you have to go to the City institutions to raise capital, you need collateral; and with the backing of a public company, like Caspian, you obviously have more chance of succeeding".

There are other initiatives in the pipeline, as one might expect from such a dynamic business. One idea put forward by Caspian chairman Chris Akers was a pay-per-view service on the Internet, transmitting games live to fans worldwide: a magnificent concept inspired by the enormous success of United's Clubcall line, which attracts more callers than any other in the Premiership.

Alas, the idea has had to be shelved due to fierce opposition from Sky TV and the other clubs in the Premiership who refuse to be party to any scheme which might upset the agreement with the satellite TV network, which currently ties them up until 2001.

## All change upstairs

Keith Handy, United's new commercial manager, is full of optimism. "The summer of 1997 was a period of change for the club", he says. "We changed our Chairman; the Chief Executive has gone; we have a new MD and a different structure, including a new operations director, new commercial director and a completely new commercial team, from myself through to Joanne Reynolds, the business development manager, and Loraine Tempest, commercial administrator.

"So literally everything is new. and in corporate terms it has gone extremely well. We have sold all 55 executive boxes, for the first time in a decade, and we have had to turn away the casual enquirers who have tried to book a box for two or three games. From that point of view, local business reaction has been superb.

"It is encouraging, because it follows a mediocre season on the pitch. When I was first appointed after going to America with the team I thought it would be difficult. We did what we had to do – stay in the Premiership – but I thought it would be tough. Okay, it still is, but people in the city have reacted extremely well towards us.

"All we can do is try and enhance our facilities, enhance our image – be a bit more personable, smile – and it seems to have worked up to now. Hopefully we can continue, and make our clients' day in and around the game a better one.

"We just deal with the corporate side, and some people suggest commercial managers are only interested in the brass: that they don't care for people. But in many ways we do, because without the corporate side ordinary fans would not see the star players on the field. This is where the income to pay for them derives from. The more successful we are, the better it is for all the club's supporters."

Keith, a former player with Bury, Manchester City, Swansea City, Grimsby Town, Huddersfield Town and Rochdale, can rightly claim to know the game at all levels. "I understand when I hear someone say the game is being taken away from the people", he says. "As a traditionalist who has played football at lower levels and been commercial manager at two lower-level clubs, Huddersfield and Bradford City, I don't like that either. I do feel for the traditions of the game. But I believe we are providing a service to everyone. You have to cater for the market-place, and the corporate side of football is in great demand. If we sell out there, we have created more income to make the club more competitive in the transfer market. It is a vicious circle, but you need corporates not only to maintain the standard of the club but to improve it".

**What she really, really wants: Spice Girl Mel B adores United**

With plenty to look forward to in the future, Leeds United also have much to be proud of from the past. Elland Road was brought up to the highest standard to become one of the venues for Euro '96, while the new training complex at Wetherby, opened in 1996, provides superb training facilities including grass and all-weather pitches, floodlighting, treatment room and offices, plus a hostel which accommodates 26 young footballers.

Like all top teams, United have their famous followers. Amongst the star supporters at the moment are top pop group James and Liz Dawn, who plays Vera Duckworth in ITV's famous soap Coronation Street, while former Elland Road heroes such as John Charles, Allan Clarke and Norman Hunter are regular guests. Another big boost came when The Spice Girls burst on to the pop scene: though she isn't often able to make it to Elland Road, "Scary Spice" Mel B is a huge Leeds United fan.

# Chapter 11

# Wars of the Roses

**Ever since Richard, Duke of York, first drew steel against the Lancastrians in the 1460s, the Wars of the Roses have raged.**

It might not be so brutal or dangerous these days, but the passions roused by the White Rose of York and the Red Rose of Lancaster nonetheless run just as deep as the Pennine range which separates these two proud counties – though the sword and axe have now been replaced by duels of a more sporting kind.

Such has been Leeds' dominance of football in the Ridings that except for Sheffield Wednesday's 1991 League Cup win, United are the only Yorkshire club to have won any of the three major trophies in English football in the past 60 years.

So it is not just history that sees Leeds' biggest rivalries coming not from the same county but from the opposite side of the Pennines. In particular, two teams from the Red Rose county have been thorns in Leeds' side; Manchester United and Liverpool.

In the Don Revie era, it was undoubtedly the Merseysiders who provided the stiffest and most passionate opposition, However, when an overall look is taken, it is with Manchester United that the rivalry has been most intense and fervent.

The first four meetings were in Division Two after Manchester were relegated in 1922, and ended in two draws and two defeats for Leeds.

It was not until the Reds had joined Leeds in Division One that the Yorkshiremen tasted success, Russell Wainscot and Tom Jennings scoring the goals in a 2–0 win on 3 October 1925.

Leeds enjoyed continued success in the 1920s and early '30s, but after that the games became more infrequent as one or the other found themselves in the second division.

Things changed in the 1960s when Don Revie took over as team manager. He led Leeds back into Division One and United enjoyed their longest spell as one of the glamour clubs of English football.

## Knockout joy and despair

Leeds enjoyed real domination in the Don Revie era and United's first two FA Cup Final trips, in 1965 and 1970, contained semi-final victories over the Reds. The two wins were amazingly similar: in 1965 Billy Bremner scored the only goal of the replay after the first game had ended in stalemate. Five years later, as United chased glory on three fronts, the Reds became a major hindrance, forcing a pair of scoreless draws before Bremner again scored the only goal of the second replay.

In recent times Manchester have held the edge in cup ties, winning another semi-final in 1977. When Leeds pipped Manchester for the 1992 League Championship, it was the Reds who dominated in knock-out games, ending United's interest in both the League and FA Cup.

It was the second consecutive year that Leeds' League Cup aspirations had ended at the hands of Manchester, 0–1 and 1–2 in the semi-final. The most recent cup meeting came in 1995 when the Reds ended Leeds' Wembley dreams in the fifth round, 3–1 at Elland Road.

In fact, the balance of power has been on the Lancashire side for a considerable spell and this makes successes for the White Rose county even more pleasurable when they come.

# Into the Premiership

United carried the League Championship banner into Old Trafford on 6 September 1992, in quite a confident mood.

Admittedly the team had not exactly fired on all cylinders yet, apart from a 5–0 trouncing of Tottenham Hotspur, but it had only lost one of its first six Premiership encounters and had a fairly settled side.

Lukic was in goal; Fairclough and Whyte formed the central defensive pairing, with Dorigo on the left and Newsome to the right. The midfield looked balanced, as good as any in fact, with Batty providing the bite, McAllister the guile, Speed the pace and Cantona, in his first appearance at Old Trafford, adding his Gallic flair and imagination to support the attack of Chapman and Wallace.

But it all went wrong; and even though Strachan and Hodge were called from the substitutes' bench, Leeds had to return over the Pennines with a 2–0 defeat ringing in their ears.

A shut-out in the return game the following February earned a vital point and lifted spirits following a 1–0 defeat at Wimbledon.

This Monday-night game, shown live on TV, had been hyped up tremendously by the media with the focus on Eric Cantona, who was now wearing the red shirt of Manchester exactly 12 months to the day after making his Leeds debut. As it turned out, however, the Frenchman was frustrated by Leeds' solid defence and neither team had the cutting edge to break through the opposition's rearguard.

# Cantona locked up

New Year's Day was as good a time as any for Leeds to re-establish their credentials as a top-class side, and this performance at Old Trafford was very reminiscent of the early Revie days when most of the credit was showered on brave and resolute defenders who gave not an inch.

Manchester were lording it some dozen points clear at the top of the table but, just as Revie had done, Howard Wilkinson prepared a battle-plan to frustrate and tease the sophisticated champions.

Leeds' approach was unashamedly to contain and smother the opposition and look for an opportunity to hit on the break. It wasn't pretty, it wasn't particularly exciting – but it was totally effective.

Chris Fairclough was released from his regular central defensive duties to shadow Cantona. So effective was he in this respect that the big Frenchman hardly got a kick, and eventually resorted to showing his mean streak.

Twice, in a matter of minutes, Fairclough felt the Frenchman's studs dig deep into his flesh. It was arro-

**Gary Kelly watches Ryan Giggs during the 0–0 draw on New Year's Day**

gantly reckless and incurred the referee's disapproval.

Giggs, on the other hand, had a better time of it against young Kelly. The Irishman resorted to holding back his tormentor when Kanchelskis had put the Welshman clean through.

But what attacks he did manage to orchestrate generally floundered on United's rock-like defence. Such was their success that goalkeeper Beeney had few chances to exploit his athleticism and the Manchester attack, which had plundered 100 goals in 1993, opened 1994 with a blank sheet.

The honours went to the defence; to the midfield, where McAllister got the better of Robson; and to Wilkinson for a tactical triumph.

Indeed, Leeds nearly snatched victory when Cantona bundled McAllister over, and the free kick was a real teaser, Fairclough rising perfectly to head goalwards, his effort kissing the outer frame of Schmeichel's goal.

No doubt this clash was a moral victory for Leeds and their fans. Yet by the end of the 1993–94 League campaign, United found themselves reflecting on four successive Roses Premiership games in which they had failed to score a single goal: in a situation reminiscent of the two sides' first four meetings in the 1920s, Leeds were again left pondering on two draws (both 0–0) and two defeats (2–0 on each occasion): not much to show for all that sweat and planning.

**1 JANUARY 1994**

**FA Carling Premiership**
Old Trafford

**Manchester United (0) 0**
**Leeds United (0) 0**

**Man Utd:**
Schmeichel; Parker, Irwin, Bruce, Pallister; Robson, Cantona, Kanchelskis, McClair, Keane; Giggs

**Leeds Utd:**
Beeney; Kelly, Dorigo, White, Fairclough, Newsome; Strachan, Pemberton, Deane, McAllister, Hodge (Sharpe)

**Att:** 44,724

United had played four London clubs when they prepared for the visit of Manchester United for the first home fixture of September 1994. It was to be a memorable match and an important result, delivering United's first League win over the Reds for 13 years.

# Reds roasted

**David Wetherall adds his name to the scoresheet against the Reds. 11 September 1994**

The after-match celebrations told it all. One Leeds fan knelt to kiss the turf after his heroes had left, to a standing ovation. United had not just beaten the champions 2–0: they had taken them apart, in a high-octane match fuelled by the passion of 39,000 ecstatic fans.

Fergie's team actually got off lightly. They might well have been three down by the interval after United had made the perfect start. Gary Speed failed to connect with White's diving header but the ball rebounded off Bruce and fell to Wetherall. The defender possibly rushed his shot: anyway, he mis-hit it through a ruck of bodies and was delighted to see the ball nestling in the net.

The men from Manchester were stunned and began to rock as McAllister, orchestrating with pin-point passes, prized them apart. In the space of two minutes Leeds created three point-blank openings – and missed them all. Masinga, Deane (a 31st-minute substitute for White) and Whelan were the culprits.

Three minutes into the second half, Deane scored. Whelan despatched the ball into the box after a ricochet from Kanchelskis had dropped in his path. He left Pallister and May for dead before picking out Deane who could not miss from two yards.

Once more Cantona got nasty, and how he escaped even a yellow card for a terrible two-footed lunge at McAllister only referee David Elleray knows. The official was on his own, too, when he amazingly awarded Manchester a penalty in the 74th minute, coolly converted by Cantona. At 2–1 Manchester had a lifeline, and almost grasped it in injury time when a cross found the head of Bruce just two yards out: but for once Mr Reliable headed wide.

That was the 13th Roses match under Howard Wilkinson's stewardship, and his first victory. A 0–0 draw at Old Trafford the following April virtually killed Manchester's hopes of retaining the title.

**11 SEPTEMBER 1994**

**FA Carling Premiership**
Elland Road

**Leeds United (1) 2**
(Wetherall, Deane)

**Manchester United (0) 1**
(Cantona, pen)

**Leeds Utd:**
Lukic; Kelly, Palmer, Wetherall, Worthington, White (Deane), McAllister, Speed, Wallace, Masinga (Fairclough), Whelan

**Man Utd:**
Schmeichel; May, Bruce, Pallister, Irwin, Kanchelskis, McClair (Butt), Ince, Giggs (Sharpe), Hughes, Cantona

**Att:** 39,120

# *On track*

Both sides slugged themselves to a standstill in a traditionally tough exchange. The pressure seemed to be getting to Schmeichel, for the giant Dane – still to concede a goal at home that year – looked alarmingly vulnerable when he dropped a Rod Wallace drive on the stroke of half-time and only just scooped the ball away from the lurking Yeboah.

Three minutes into the second half and Denmark's Number One gifted United another chance when he kicked a clearance straight at Carlton Palmer. The ball looped back over the 'keeper's head and bounced on the goal-line, but the look of panic on his face soon turned to relief as the backspin enabled him to grab the ball.

At the other end, Lukic broke Cole's heart when he darted off his line to save bravely and was perfectly positioned to deal with a powerfully-struck angled shot from Manchester's £7 million striker. With five minutes to go, Ince struck a real pile-driver that looked a winner all the way – until Weatherall flung himself in its path and deflected the ball over the bar to keep United on track for a UEFA Cup place.

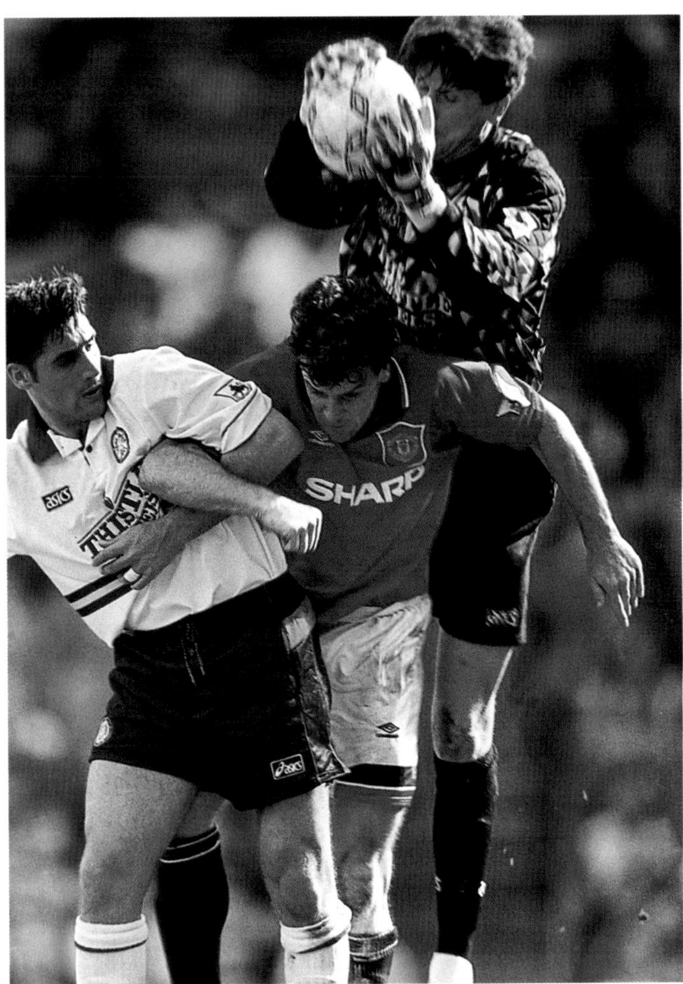


**John Lukic claims the ball from Mark Hughes' head as John Pemberton lends a hand**

**2 APRIL 1995**

**FA Carling Premiership**
Old Trafford

**Manchester United (0) 0,**
**Leeds United (0) 0**

**Man Utd:**
Schmeichel; Neville, Keane, Pallister, Irwin, Beckham, McClair, Ince, Giggs; Hughes, Cole

**Leeds Utd:**
Lukic; Kelly, Wetherall, Pemberton, Dorigo, Wallace (Whelan), Palmer, McAllister, Couzens, Yeboah, Deane (Worthington)

**Att:**
43,712

Leeds got an early Christmas present in 1995 when a Sunday Christmas Eve was enlivened by a visit from Manchester. It wasn't so much a case of Manchester United coming to Elland Road bearing gifts as another thoroughly professional performance from the Yorkshiremen which sent Alex Ferguson's men back across the Pennines without a point. The day was cold, but the atmosphere was white-hot and most of the 39,801 fans went home warmed by what they had witnessed.

Neither team was enjoying a good run of form; indeed, both were looking for their first victory in December. Leeds had suffered three defeats and a draw, while Manchester had been marginally more successful with three draws and a loss. But Leeds were smarting from their previous match, an embarrassing 6–2 defeat at the hands of Yorkshire rivals Sheffield Wednesday.

It took just six minutes for the home side to take the lead when Gary McAllister converted a penalty. The lead lasted until the half-hour mark, when Andy Cole snatched an equalizer after a defensive slip. Eight minutes before half-time, Tony Yeboah struck a brilliant second goal to give Leeds the lead again.

The second half was great to watch for Leeds fans as the Reds struggled to hold on to the game. Schmeichel was constantly in action as the Manchester defence was dragged this way and that. Tomas Brolin had one of his more effective games and it was he who set up Brian Deane for the final goal, 17 minutes from time.

**24 DECEMBER 1995**

**FA Carling Premiership**
Elland Road

**Leeds United (2) 3**
(McAllister, Yeboah, Deane)
**Manchester United (1) 1**
(Cole)

**Man Utd:**
Schmeichel; Neville, Keane, Pallister, Irwin, Beckham, McClair, Ince, Giggs; Hughes, Cole

**Leeds Utd:**
Beeney; Kelly, Dorigo, Palmer, Wetherall, Jobson, Brolin, Yeboah (Wallace), Deane, McAllister, Speed

The only surprise about Manchester's 1–0 triumph at Old Trafford in April was the closeness of the score. United came into this game on the back of three successive League defeats in which they had conceded nine goals. Beeney replaced Lukic for this one; Beesley was preferred to Pemberton and Worthington came into Gray's left wing-back position.

## *Wilko and out*

Manchester United absolutely destroyed a transitional Leeds team to deliver a K-O blow which spelled the end of Howard Wilkinson's career at Elland Road.

Adopting a fluid 4-5-1 formation, Manchester attacked relentlessly. Wilkinson had talked before the kick-off of going hard at the Reds, but the truth is they found themselves a goal down in two minutes and were never able to pick themselves up.

The goal had a hint of farce about it: Ronnie Johnsen was allowed a free header from Karel Poborsky's corner and headed down in textbook fashion. Mark Ford hacked it off the line but gave it back to Johnsen, who had another go. This time Ian Harte, on the line, got his boot to the ball, but only succeeded in driving it into Nigel Martyn's back, from which the ball rebounded into the net.

That was the only goal of the half and was quite remarkable considering Manchester's domination. Martyn made a world-class save when he tipped a cracker from Nicky Butt over the bar, and then survived a penalty when, to the delight of the home fans who once idolized him, Eric Cantona shot wide.

The smiles turned to groans when, three minutes into the second half, Butt made it 2–0. Poborsky paved the way thanks to two half-hearted challenges and Butt, maintaining great composure, slipped the ball inside the post as Martyn came out to challenge.

From then on it was only a matter of how many. Only goalkeeper Martyn offered any true resistance, another fingertip save from David Beckham being the pick of his contribution before Cantona set Poborsky free to lash the ball past the unfortunate custodian. Leeds did muster a rally in the closing phase of the match and might have scored, but Harte shot wide and on-loan veteran Mark Hateley could not make his header count.

Ironically, it was Cantona who drove the last nail in Wilkinson's coffin, side-footing Ole Gunnar Solskjaer's cross into the net in the final minute.

It was another Christmas-time fixture when Leeds travelled to Manchester for the return fixture in

**7 SEPTEMBER 1996**

**FA Carling Premiership**
Elland Road

**Leeds United (0) 0**
**Manchester United (1) 4**
(Martyn o.g., Butt, Poborsky, Cantona, pen)

**Leeds Utd:**
Martyn; Kelly, Palmer, Wetherall, Sharpe, Wallace (Hateley), Rush, Bowyer (Radebe), Jobson, Harte, Ford (Gray)

**Man Utd:**
Schmeichel; Neville G., Irwin, May, Poborsky (Solskjaer), Johnsen, Cantona, Butt, Beckham (McClair), Giggs, Cruyff (Cole)

**Att:** 39,694

1996–97. George Graham had been in charge for just over three months and Leeds' form had shown little sign of improving. The defence was much more solid, but the goals had all but dried up. Indeed, the previous four matches had brought three goalless draws and a 3–1 defeat at home to relegation-haunted Coventry. Manchester had just thumped nine goals past Sunderland and Nottingham Forest and were brimming with confidence.

The crowd of 55,256 were in expectant mood and Graham decided that the best hope of controlling the Reds was to assign Radebe to man-mark Cantona and by stifling him to throw Manchester off their stride.

The meticulous plan was in tatters inside nine minutes as the Reds swept the length of the pitch. Denis Irwin played a long downfield pass to Cantona, who flicked the ball into the path of Ryan Giggs. As the Welsh winger sped into the penalty area his run was unceremoniously halted by Gary Kelly – and up stepped Cantona to deliver his parting gift from the penalty spot.

Manchester continued to dominate the proceedings, but they were unable to add to their tally. As a Liverpool player, Ian Rush had found goals against Manchester United harder to come by than any other opponent, and he found the Reds' defence in typically uncharitable mood.

The final battle of 1996 belonged to Manchester, but the Wars of the Roses rumble on and in their stronghold east of the Pennines United watch and wait, in the knowledge that their day will come again.

**Tony Yeboah exploits his power and strength against Johnsen in the last battle of 1996**

**28 DECEMBER 1996**

**FA Carling Premiership**
Old Trafford

**Manchester United (1) 1**
(Cantona, pen)
**Leeds United (0) 0**

**Man Utd:**
Schmeichel, Neville G., Irwin, Keane, May, Johnsen, Cantona, Butt (McClair), Beckham, Giggs (Poborsky), Solskjaer (Cole)

**Leeds Utd:**
Martyn, Kelly, Radebe, Palmer, Halle, Dorigo, Jackson, Yeboah (Gray), Rush, Deane, Bowyer

**Att:** 55,256

# Chapter 12

# The Records

## Year-by-year statistics

### Season 1992–93

| FA CUP | | | | | |
|---|---|---|---|---|---|
| **Date** | **Team** | **Venue** | **Att** | **Score** | **Scorer** |
| **3rd Round** | | | | | |
| 2 Jan | Charlton Athletic | H | 21,287 | 1–1 | Speed |
| **3rd Round REPLAY** | | | | | |
| 13 Jan | Charlton Athletic | A | 8,337 | 3–1 | Speed, Garland, McAllister |
| **4th Round** | | | | | |
| 25 Jan | Arsenal | A | 26,516 | 2–2 | Speed, Chapman |
| **4th Round REPLAY** | | | | | |
| 3 Feb | Arsenal | H | 26,449 | 2–3 | Shutt, McAllister |

| COCA-COLA CUP | | | | | |
|---|---|---|---|---|---|
| **Date** | **Team** | **Venue** | **Att** | **Score** | **Scorer** |
| **2nd Round** | | | | | |
| 1st L 22 Sept | Scunthorpe U | H | 10,113 | 4–1 | Strachan, Chapman, Speed, Shutt |
| 2nd L 27 Oct | Scunthorpe U | A | 7,419 | 2–2 | Wallace, Chapman |
| **3rd Round** | | | | | |
| 10 Nov | Watford | A | 18,035 | 1–2 | McAllister |

| PLAYER APPEARANCES | | | | | |
|---|---|---|---|---|---|
| **Name** | **App** | **(Sub)** | **Gls** | **Coca-Cola Cup Goals** | **FA Cup Goals** |
| Lukic | 39 | | | | |
| Newsome | 30 | 7 | | | |
| Dorigo | 33 | | | | |
| Batty | 30 | | 1 | | |
| Fairclough | 29 | 1 | 3 | | |
| Whyte | 34 | | 1 | | |
| Cantona | 12 | 1 | 6 | | |
| Wallace, Rob | 31 | 1 | 7 | 1 | |
| Chapman | 36 | 4 | 13 | 2 | 1 |
| McAllister | 32 | | 5 | 1 | 2 |
| Speed | 39 | | 7 | 1 | 3 |
| Strachan | 25 | 6 | 4 | 1 | |
| Hodge | 9 | 14 | 2 | | |
| Sellars | 6 | 1 | | | |
| Wetherall | 13 | | 1 | | |
| Shutt | 6 | 8 | | 1 | 1 |
| Rocastle | 11 | 7 | 1 | | |
| Day | 2 | | | | |
| Wallace, Ray | 5 | 1 | | | |
| Varadi | 2 | 2 | 1 | | |
| Sterland | 3 | | | | |
| Strandli | 5 | 5 | 2 | | |
| Bowman | 3 | 1 | | | |
| Kerslake | 8 | | | | |
| Forrester | 5 | 1 | | | |
| Kerr | 3 | 2 | | | |
| Tinkler | 5 | 2 | | | |
| Sharp | 4 | | | | |
| Whelan | 1 | | | | |
| Beeney | 1 | | | | |

| FA PREMIER LEAGUE | | | | | |
|---|---|---|---|---|---|
| **Date** | **Team** | **Venue** | **Att** | **Score** | **Scorer** |
| 15 Aug | Wimbledon | H | 25,795 | 2–1 | Chapman 2 |
| 19 Aug | Aston Villa | A | 29,151 | 1–1 | Speed |
| 22 Aug | Middlesbrough | A | 18,649 | 1–4 | Cantona |
| 25 Aug | Tottenham Hotspur | H | 28,218 | 5–0 | Wallace, Cantona 3, Chapman |
| 29 Aug | Liverpool | H | 29,597 | 2–2 | McAllister, Chapman |
| 1 Sept | Oldham Athletic | A | 13,848 | 2–2 | Cantona 2 |
| 6 Sept | Manchester United | A | 31,296 | 0–2 | |
| 13 Sept | Aston Villa | H | 27,817 | 1–1 | Hodge |
| 19 Sept | Southampton | A | 16,229 | 1–1 | Speed |
| 26 Sept | Everton | H | 27,915 | 2–0 | McAllister (pen), Chapman |
| 3 Oct | Ipswich Town | A | 21,200 | 2–4 | Stockwell (og), Speed |
| 17 Oct | Sheffield United | H | 29,706 | 3–1 | Chapman, Speed, Whyte |
| 24 Oct | QPR | A | 19,326 | 1–2 | Strachan |
| 31 Oct | Coventry City | H | 28,018 | 2–2 | Strachan, Fairclough |
| 7 Nov | Manchester City | A | 27,255 | 0–4 | |
| 21 Nov | Arsenal | H | 30,516 | 3–0 | Fairclough, Chapman, McAllister |
| 29 Nov | Chelsea | A | 24,345 | 0–1 | |
| 5 Dec | Nottingham Forest | H | 29,364 | 1–4 | Speed |
| 12 Dec | Sheffield Wednesday | H | 29,770 | 3–1 | Speed, Chapman, Varadi |
| 20 Dec | Crystal Palace | A | 14,462 | 0–1 | |
| 26 Dec | Blackburn Rovers | A | 19,910 | 1–3 | McAllister |
| 28 Dec | Norwich City | H | 30,282 | 0–0 | |
| 9 Jan | Southampton | H | 26,071 | 2–1 | Chapman, Speed |
| 16 Jan | Everton | A | 21,031 | 0–2 | |
| 30 Jan | Middlesbrough | H | 30,344 | 3–0 | Strandli, Batty, Fairclough |
| 6 Feb | Wimbledon | A | 6,704 | 0–1 | |
| 8 Feb | Manchester United | H | 34,166 | 0–0 | |
| 13 Feb | Oldham Athletic | H | 27,654 | 2–0 | McAllister (pen), Chapman |
| 20 Feb | Tottenham Hotspur | A | 32,040 | 0–4 | |
| 24 Feb | Arsenal | A | 21,061 | 0–0 | |
| 27 Feb | Ipswich Town | H | 28,848 | 1–0 | Dorigo (pen) |
| 13 Mar | Manchester City | H | 30,840 | 1–0 | Rocastle |
| 21 Mar | Nottingham Forest | A | 25,148 | 1–1 | Wallace |
| 24 Mar | Chelsea | H | 28,135 | 1–1 | Wetherall |
| 6 Apr | Sheffield United | A | 20,562 | 1–2 | Strandli |
| 10 Apr | Blackburn Rovers | H | – | 5–2 | Strachan 3 (2 pen), Wallace, Chapman |
| 14 Apr | Norwich City | A | 18,613 | 2–4 | Chapman, Wallace |
| 17 Apr | Crystal Palace | H | 27,545 | 0–0 | |
| 21 Apr | Liverpool | A | 34,992 | 0–2 | |
| 1 May | QPR | H | 31,408 | 1–1 | Hodge |
| 4 May | Sheffield Wednesday | A | 26,855 | 1–1 | King (og) |
| 8 May | Coventry City | A | 19,591 | 3–3 | Wallace 3 |

Final League Position : 17

## Season 1993–94

| FA PREMIER LEAGUE | | | | | |
|---|---|---|---|---|---|
| **Date** | **Team** | **Venue** | **Att** | **Score** | **Scorer** |
| 14 Aug | Manchester City | A | 32,266 | 1–1 | Deane |
| 17 Aug | West Ham United | H | 34,588 | 1–0 | Speed |
| 21 Aug | Norwich City | H | 32,008 | 0–4 | |
| 24 Aug | Arsenal | A | 29,042 | 1–2 | Strachan |
| 28 Aug | Liverpool | A | 44,068 | 0–2 | |
| 30 Aug | Oldham Athletic | H | 28,717 | 1–0 | Strachan |
| 11 Sept | Southampton | A | 13,511 | 2–0 | Deane, Speed |
| 18 Sept | Sheffield United | H | 33,879 | 2–1 | McAllister, Strachan |
| 25 Sept | Coventry City | A | 13,933 | 2–0 | Wallace 2 |
| 2 Oct | Wimbledon | H | 30,255 | 4–0 | Speed 2, McAllister 2 |
| 17 Oct | Ipswich Town | A | 17,532 | 0–0 | |
| 23 Oct | Blackburn Rovers | H | 37,827 | 3–3 | McAllister (pen), Newsome, og |
| 30 Oct | Sheffield Wednesday | A | 31,892 | 3–3 | Fairclough, Wallace, Speed |
| 6 Nov | Chelsea | H | 35,050 | 4–1 | Deane, Wallace 2, Rocastle |
| 20 Nov | Tottenham Hotspur | A | 31,275 | 1–1 | Deane |
| 23 Nov | Everton | A | 17,102 | 1–1 | Wallace |
| 27 Nov | Swindon Town | H | 32,630 | 3–0 | Deane, Wallace, Speed |
| 4 Dec | Manchester City | H | 33,820 | 3–2 | Wallace, Speed, Deane |
| 8 Dec | West Ham United | A | 20,468 | 1–0 | Wallace |
| 13 Dec | Norwich City | A | 16,586 | 1–2 | Wallace |
| 18 Dec | Arsenal | H | 37,289 | 2–1 | McAllister, Adams (og) |
| 22 Dec | Newcastle United | A | 36,388 | 1–1 | Fairclough |
| 29 Dec | QPR | H | 39,124 | 1–1 | Hodge |
| 1 Jan | Manchester United | A | 44,724 | 0–0 | |
| 15 Jan | Ipswich Town | H | 31,317 | 0–0 | |
| 23 Jan | Blackburn Rovers | A | 17,475 | 1–2 | Speed |
| 6 Feb | Aston Villa | A | 26,919 | 0–1 | |
| 19 Feb | Liverpool | H | 40,029 | 2–0 | Wetherall, McAllister |
| 28 Feb | Oldham Athletic | A | 11,136 | 1–1 | McAllister |
| 5 Mar | Southampton | H | 30,829 | 0–0 | |
| 13 Mar | Sheffield United | A | 19,425 | 2–2 | Speed, Deane |
| 16 Mar | Aston Villa | H | 33,126 | 2–0 | Wallace, Deane |
| 19 Mar | Coventry City | H | 30,023 | 1–0 | Wallace |
| 26 Mar | Wimbledon | A | 9,035 | 0–1 | |
| 1 Apr | Newcastle United | H | 40,005 | 1–1 | Fairclough |
| 4 Apr | QPR | A | 15,365 | 4–0 | Deane, Wallace |
| 17 Apr | Tottenham Hotspur | H | 33,658 | 2–0 | Wallace 2 |
| 23 Apr | Chelsea | A | 18,544 | 1–1 | Speed |
| 27 Apr | Manchester United | H | 41,127 | 0–2 | |
| 30 Apr | Everton | H | 35,487 | 3–0 | McAllister, Watson (og), White |
| 3 May | Sheffield Wednesday | H | 33,575 | 2–2 | White, Wallace |
| 7 May | Swindon Town | A | 17,228 | 5–0 | Deane 2, Wallace, White, Fairclough |
| Final League Position: 5 | | | | | |

| PLAYER APPEARANCES | | | | | |
|---|---|---|---|---|---|
| **Name** | **App** | **(Sub)** | **Gls** | **Coca-Cola Cup Goals** | **FA Cup Goals** |
| Lukic | 20 | | | | |
| Kelly | 42 | | | | |
| Dorigo | 37 | | | | |
| Batty | 8 | 1 | | | |
| Fairclough | 40 | | 4 | | |
| O'Leary | 10 | | | | |
| Strachan | 32 | 1 | 3 | | 1 |
| Whelan | 6 | 10 | | 1 | |
| Deane | 41 | | 11 | | 1 |
| McAllister | 42 | | 8 | | |
| Speed | 35 | 1 | 10 | 1 | 1 |
| Wallace, Rod | 34 | 3 | 17 | | |
| Newsome | 25 | 4 | 1 | | |
| Beeney | 22 | | | | |
| Wetherall | 31 | 1 | 1 | | 1 |
| Strandli | | 4 | | | |
| Rocastle | 6 | 1 | 1 | | |
| Hodge | 7 | 1 | 1 | | |
| Pemberton | 6 | 3 | | | |
| Forrester | 2 | 1 | | | 2 |
| Sharp | 7 | 3 | | | |
| Wallace, Ray | 0 | 1 | | | |
| White | 9 | 6 | 5 | | 1 |
| Tinkler | 0 | 3 | | | |
| Ford | 0 | 1 | | | |

| COCA-COLA CUP | | | | | |
|---|---|---|---|---|---|
| **Date** | **Team** | **Venue** | **Att** | **Score** | **Scorer** |
| **2nd Round** | | | | | |
| 1st L 21 Sept | Sunderland | A | 17,101 | 1–2 | Speed |
| 2nd L 6 Oct | Sunderland | H | 22,165 | 1–2 | Whelan |

| FA CUP | | | | | |
|---|---|---|---|---|---|
| **Date** | **Team** | **Venue** | **Att** | **Score** | **Scorer** |
| **3rd Round** | | | | | |
| 8 Jan | Crewe Alex | H | 23,475 | 3–1 | Deane, Forrester 2 |
| **4th Round** | | | | | |
| 29 Jan | Oxford U | A | 11,029 | 2–2 | Speed, Wetherall |
| **4th Round REPLAY** | | | | | |
| 9 Feb | Oxford U | H | 22,167 | 2–3 | Strachan, White |

## Season 1994–95

| FA PREMIER LEAGUE | | | | | |
|---|---|---|---|---|---|
| **Date** | **Team** | **Venue** | **Att** | **Score** | **Scorer** |
| 20 Aug | West Ham United | A | 18,610 | 0–0 | |
| 23 Aug | Arsenal | H | 34,318 | 1–0 | Whelan |
| 27 Aug | Chelsea | H | 32,212 | 2–3 | Masinga, Whelan |
| 30 Aug | Crystal Palace | A | 14,453 | 2–1 | White, Whelan |
| 11 Sept | Manchester United | H | 39,120 | 2–1 | Wetherall, Deane |
| 17 Sept | Coventry City | A | 15,383 | 1–2 | Speed |
| 26 Sept | Sheffield Wednesday | A | 23,227 | 1–1 | McAllister |
| 1 Oct | Manchester City | H | 30,938 | 2–0 | Whelan 2 |
| 8 Oct | Norwich City | A | 17,390 | 1–2 | Wallace |
| 15 Oct | Tottenham Hotspur | H | 39,362 | 1–1 | Deane |
| 24 Oct | Leicester City | H | 28,479 | 2–1 | McAllister, Whelan |
| 29 Oct | Southampton | A | 15,202 | 3–1 | Wallace 2, Maddison (og) |
| 1 Nov | Ipswich Town | A | 15,534 | 0–2 | |
| 5 Nov | Wimbledon | H | 27,246 | 3–1 | Wetherall, White, Speed |
| 19 Nov | QPR | A | 17,416 | 2–3 | McDonald (og), Deane |
| 26 Nov | Nottingham Forest | H | 37,709 | 1–0 | Whelan |
| 5 Dec | Everton | A | 25,906 | 0–3 | |
| 10 Dec | West Ham United | H | 28,987 | 2–2 | Worthington, Deane |
| 17 Dec | Arsenal | A | 38,100 | 3–1 | Masinga 2, Deane |
| 26 Dec | Newcastle United | H | 39,337 | 0–0 | |
| 31 Dec | Liverpool | H | 38,468 | 0–2 | |
| 2 Jan | Aston Villa | A | 35,038 | 0–0 | |
| 14 Jan | Southampton | H | 28,969 | 0–0 | |
| 24 Jan | QPR | H | 28,750 | 4–0 | Masinga 2, White, Deane |
| 1 Feb | Blackburn Rovers | A | 28,561 | 1–1 | McAllister (pen) |
| 4 Feb | Wimbledon | A | 10,211 | 0–0 | |
| 22 Feb | Everton | H | 30,793 | 1–0 | Yeboah |
| 25 Feb | Manchester City | A | 22,892 | 0–0 | |
| 4 Mar | Sheffield Wednesday | H | 33,774 | 0–1 | |
| 11 Mar | Chelsea | A | 20,174 | 3–0 | Yeboah 2, McAllister |
| 15 Mar | Leicester City | A | 20,068 | 3–1 | Yeboah 2, Palmer |
| 18 Mar | Coventry City | H | 29,231 | 3–1 | Wallace, Yeboah, Gould (og) |
| 22 Mar | Nottingham Forest | A | 26,299 | 0–3 | |
| 2 Apr | Manchester United | A | 43,712 | 0–0 | |
| 5 Apr | Ipswich Town | H | 28,565 | 4–0 | Speed, Yeboah 3 |
| 9 Apr | Liverpool | A | 37,454 | 1–0 | Deane |
| 15 Apr | Blackburn Rovers | H | 39,426 | 1–1 | Deane |
| 17 Apr | Newcastle United | A | 35,626 | 2–1 | Yeboah, McAllister (pen) |
| 29 Apr | Aston Villa | H | 32,973 | 1–0 | Palmer |
| 6 May | Norwich City | H | 31,981 | 21 | McAllister (pen), Palmer |
| 9 May | Crystal Palace | H | 30,963 | 3–1 | Yeboah 2, Wetherall |
| 14 May | Tottenham Hotspur | A | 33,040 | 1–1 | Deane |
| Final League Position: 5 | | | | | |

| PLAYER APPEARANCES | | | | | |
|---|---|---|---|---|---|
| **Name** | **App** | **(Sub)** | **Gls** | **Coca-Cola Cup Goals** | **FA Cup Goals** |
| Lukic | 42 | | | | |
| Kelly | 42 | | | | |
| Worthington | 21 | 6 | 1 | | |
| Palmer | 39 | | 3 | | 1 |
| Wetherall | 38 | | 3 | | 2 |
| White | 18 | 5 | 3 | | 1 |
| Strachan | 5 | 1 | | | |
| Wallace, Rod | 30 | 2 | 4 | | |
| Deane | 33 | 2 | 9 | | 1 |
| McAllister | 41 | | 6 | | |
| Speed | 39 | | 3 | | |
| Masinga | 15 | 7 | 5 | | 4 |
| Whelan | 18 | 5 | 7 | | |
| Fairclough | 1 | 4 | | | |
| Pemberton | 22 | 5 | | | |
| Tinkler | 3 | | | | |
| Radebe | 9 | 3 | | | |
| Dorigo | 28 | | | | |
| Yeboah | 16 | 2 | 12 | | 1 |
| Couzens | 2 | 2 | | | |
| Sharp | | 2 | | | |

| COCA-COLA CUP | | | | | |
|---|---|---|---|---|---|
| **Date** | **Team** | **Venue** | **Att** | **Score** | **Scorer** |
| **2nd Round** | | | | | |
| 1st L 21 Sept | Mansfield T | H | 7,844 | 0–1 | |
| 2nd L 4 Oct | Mansfield T | A | 7,227 | 0–0 | |

| FA CUP | | | | | |
|---|---|---|---|---|---|
| **Date** | **Team** | **Venue** | **Att** | **Score** | **Scorer** |
| **3rd Round** | | | | | |
| 7 Jan | Walsall | A | 8,691 | 1–1 | Wetherall |
| **3rd Round REPLAY** | | | | | |
| 17 Jan | Walsall | H | 17,881 | 5–2 | Deane, Wetherall, Masinga 3 |
| **4th Round** | | | | | |
| 28 Jan | Oldham Ath | H | 25,010 | 3–2 | White, Palmer, Masinga |
| **5th Round** | | | | | |
| 19 Feb | Man U | A | 42,744 | 1–3 | Yeboah |

## Season 1995–96

| FA PREMIER LEAGUE | | | | | |
|---|---|---|---|---|---|
| **Date** | **Team** | **Venue** | **Att** | **Score** | **Scorer** |
| 19 Aug | West Ham United | A | 22,901 | 2–1 | Yeboah 2 |
| 21 Aug | Liverpool | H | 35,852 | 1–0 | Yeboah |
| 26 Aug | Aston Villa | H | 35,086 | 2–0 | Speed, White |
| 30 Aug | Southampton | A | 15,212 | 1–1 | Dorigo |
| 9 Sept | Tottenham Hotspur | A | 30,034 | 1–2 | Yeboah |
| 16 Sept | QPR | H | 31,504 | 1–3 | Wetherall |
| 23 Sept | Wimbledon | A | 13,307 | 4–2 | Palmer, Yeboah 3 |
| 30 Sept | Sheffield Wednesday | H | 34, 076 | 2–0 | Yeboah, Speed |
| 14 Oct | Arsenal | H | 38,552 | 0–3 | |
| 21 Oct | Manchester City | A | 26,390 | 0–0 | |
| 28 Oct | Coventry City | H | 30,161 | 3–1 | McAllister 3 (1 pen) |
| 4 Nov | Middlesbrough | A | 29,467 | 1–1 | Deane |
| 18 Nov | Chelsea | H | 36,209 | 1–0 | Yeboah |
| 25 Nov | Newcastle United | A | 36,572 | 1–2 | Deane |
| 2 Dec | Manchester City | H | 33,249 | 0–1 | |
| 9 Dec | Wimbledon | H | 27,984 | 1–1 | Jobson |
| 16 Dec | Sheffield Wednesday | A | 24,573 | 2–6 | Brolin, Wallace |
| 24 Dec | Manchester United | H | 39,801 | 3–1 | McAllister (pen), Yeboah, Deane |
| 27 Dec | Bolton Wanderers | A | 18,414 | 2–0 | Brolin, Wetherall |
| 30 Dec | Everton | A | 40,009 | 0–2 | |
| 1 Jan | Blackburn Rovers | H | 31,285 | 0–0 | |
| 13 Jan | West Ham United | H | 30,658 | 2–0 | Brolin 2 |
| 20 Jan | Liverpool | A | 40,254 | 0–5 | |
| 31 Jan | Nottingham Forest | A | 35,982 | 1–2 | Palmer |
| 3 Feb | Aston Villa | A | 24,465 | 0–3 | |
| 2 Mar | Bolton Wanderers | H | 30,106 | 0–1 | |
| 6 Mar | QPR | A | 13,991 | 2–1 | Yeboah 2 |
| 13 Mar | Blackburn Rovers | A | 23,358 | 0–1 | |
| 17 Mar | Everton | H | 29,421 | 2–2 | Deane 2 |
| 29 Mar | Middlesbrough | H | 31,778 | 0–1 | |
| 3 Apr | Southampton | H | 26,077 | 1–0 | Deane |
| 6 Apr | Arsenal | A | 37,619 | 1–2 | Deane |
| 8 Apr | Nottingham Forest | H | 29,220 | 1–3 | Wetherall |
| 13 Apr | Chelsea | A | 22,131 | 1–4 | McAllister |
| 17 Apr | Manchester United | A | 48,382 | 0–1 | |
| 29 Apr | Newcastle United | H | 38,862 | 0–1 | |
| 2 May | Tottenham Hotspur | H | 30,061 | 1–3 | Wetherall |
| 5 May | Coventry City | A | 22,769 | 0–0 | |
| Final League Position: 13 | | | | | |

| PLAYER APPEARANCES | | | | | |
|---|---|---|---|---|---|
| **Name** | **App** | **(Sub)** | **Gls** | **Coca-Cola Cup Goals** | **FA Cup Goals** |
| Lukic | 28 | | | | |
| Kelly | 34 | | | | |
| Dorigo | 17 | | 1 | | |
| Palmer | 35 | | 2 | | |
| Pemberton | 16 | 1 | | | |
| Wetherall | 34 | | 4 | | |
| Deane | 30 | 4 | 7 | 2 | 1 |
| Wallace, Rod | 12 | 12 | 1 | | 1 |
| Yeboah | 22 | | 12 | 3 | 1 |
| McAllister | 36 | | 5 | 1 | 3 |
| Speed | 29 | | 2 | 3 | 1 |
| Whelan | 3 | 5 | | | |
| Beesley | 8 | 2 | | | |
| Worthington | 12 | 4 | | | |
| White | 1 | 3 | 1 | | |
| Masinga | 5 | 4 | | 2 | |
| Tinkler | 5 | 4 | | | |
| Couzens | 8 | 6 | | 1 | |
| Jobson | 12 | 1 | | | |
| Sharp | | 1 | | | |
| Ford | 12 | | | | |
| Brolin | 17 | 2 | 4 | | |
| Bowman | 1 | 2 | | | |
| Beeney | 10 | | | | |
| Radebe | 10 | 3 | | | |
| Chapman | 2 | | | | |
| Gray | 12 | 2 | | | |
| Harte | 2 | 2 | | | |
| Maybury | 1 | | | | |
| Kewell | 2 | | | | |
| Blunt | 2 | 1 | | | |
| Jackson | | 1 | | | |

| COCA-COLA CUP | | | | | |
|---|---|---|---|---|---|
| **Date** | **Team** | **Venue** | **Att** | **Score** | **Scorer** |
| **2nd Round** | | | | | |
| 1st L 19 Sept<br>2nd L 3 Oct | Notts County<br>Notts County | H<br>A | 12,384<br>12,477 | 0–0<br>3–2 | McAllister, Couzens, Speed |
| **3rd Round** | | | | | |
| 25 Oct | Derby County | A | 16,030 | 1–0 | Speed |
| **4th Round** | | | | | |
| 29 Nov | Blackburn R | H | 26,006 | 2–1 | Deane, Yeboah |
| **5th Round** | | | | | |
| 10 Jan | Reading | H | 21,023 | 2–1 | Masinga, Speed |
| **Semi-Final** | | | | | |
| 1st L 11 Feb | Birmingham C | A | 24,781 | 2–1 | Yeboah, Whyte (og) |
| 2nd L 25 Feb | Birmingham C | H | 35,435 | 3–0 | Masinga, Yeboah, Deane |
| **Final** | | | | | |
| 24 Mar | Aston Villa | A | 77,065 | 0–3 | |

| FA CUP | | | | | |
|---|---|---|---|---|---|
| **Date** | **Team** | **Venue** | **Att** | **Score** | **Scorer** |
| **3rd Round** | | | | | |
| 7 Jan | Derby C | A | 16,155 | 4–2 | Speed, Deane, McAllister, Yeboah |
| **3rd Round REPLAY** | | | | | |
| 14 Feb | Bolton W | A | 16,694 | 1–0 | Wallace |
| **4th Round** | | | | | |
| 15 Feb | Port Vale | H | 18,607 | 0–0 | |
| **4th Round REPLAY** | | | | | |
| 27 Feb | Port Vale | A | 14,023 | 2–1 | McAllister 2 |
| **5th Round** | | | | | |
| 10 Mar | Liverpool | H | 34,632 | 0–0 | |
| **5th Round REPLAY** | | | | | |
| 20 Mar | Liverpool | A | 30,812 | 0–3 | |

## Season 1996–97

| FA PREMIER LEAGUE | | | | | |
|---|---|---|---|---|---|
| **Date** | **Team** | **Venue** | **Att** | **Score** | **Scorer** |
| 17 Aug | Derby County | A | 17,927 | 3–3 | Laursen (og), Harte, Bowyer |
| 20 Aug | Sheffield Wednesday | H | 31,011 | 0–2 | |
| 26 Aug | Wimbledon | H | 25,860 | 1–0 | Sharpe |
| 4 Sept | Blackburn Rovers | A | 23,226 | 1–0 | Harte |
| 7 Sept | Manchester United | H | 39,694 | 0–4 | |
| 14 Sept | Coventry City | A | 17,297 | 1–2 | Couzens |
| 21 Sept | Newcastle United | H | 36,070 | 0–1 | |
| 28 Sept | Leicester City | A | 20,359 | 0–1 | |
| 12 Oct | Nottingham Forest | H | 29,165 | 2–0 | Wallace 2 |
| 19 Oct | Aston Villa | A | 39,051 | 0–2 | |
| 26 Oct | Arsenal | A | 38,076 | 0–3 | |
| 2 Nov | Sunderland | H | 31,667 | 3–0 | Ford, Deane, Sharpe |
| 16 Nov | Liverpool | H | 39,981 | 0–2 | |
| 23 Nov | Southampton | A | 15,241 | 2–0 | Kelly, Sharpe |
| 1 Dec | Chelsea | H | 32,671 | 2–0 | Deane, Rush |
| 7 Dec | Middlesbrough | A | 30,018 | 0–0 | |
| 14 Dec | Tottenham Hotspur | H | 33,783 | 0–0 | |
| 21 Dec | Everton | A | 36,954 | 0–0 | |
| 26 Dec | Coventry City | H | 36,465 | 1–3 | Deane |
| 28 Dec | Manchester United | A | 55,256 | 0–1 | |
| 1 Jan | Newcastle United | A | 36,489 | 0–3 | |
| 11 Jan | Leicester City | H | 29,486 | 3–0 | Bowyer, Rush 2 |
| 20 Jan | West Ham United | A | 19,441 | 2–0 | Kelly, Bowyer |
| 29 Jan | Derby County | H | 27,549 | 0–0 | |
| 1 Feb | Arsenal | H | 35,502 | 0–0 | |
| 19 Feb | Liverpool | A | 38,957 | 0–4 | |
| 22 Feb | Sunderland | A | 21,890 | 1–0 | Bowyer |
| 1 Mar | West Ham United | H | 30,575 | 1–0 | Sharpe |
| 8 Mar | Everton | H | 32,055 | 1–0 | Molenaar |
| 12 Mar | Southampton | H | 25,913 | 0–0 | |
| 15 Mar | Tottenham Hotspur | A | 33,040 | 0–1 | |
| 22 Mar | Sheffield Wednesday | A | 30,373 | 2–2 | Sharpe, Wallace |
| 7 Apr | Blackburn Rovers | H | 27,264 | 0–0 | |
| 16 Apr | Wimbledon | A | 7,979 | 0–2 | |
| 19 Apr | Nottingham Forest | A | 25,565 | 1–1 | Deane |
| 22 Apr | Aston Villa | H | 26,897 | 0–0 | |
| 3 May | Chelsea | A | 28,277 | 0–0 | |
| 11 May | Middlesbrough | H | 38,569 | 1–1 | Deane |
| Final League Position: 11 | | | | | |

| PLAYER APPEARANCES | | | | | |
|---|---|---|---|---|---|
| **Name** | **App** | **(Sub)** | **Gls** | **Coca-Cola Cup Goals** | **FA Cup Goals** |
| Martyn | 37 | | | | |
| Kelly | 33 | 2 | 2 | | |
| Couzens | 7 | 3 | 1 | | |
| Palmer | 26 | 2 | | | |
| Radebe | 28 | 4 | | | |
| Jobson | 10 | | | | |
| Sharpe | 25 | | 5 | 1 | |
| Ford | 15 | 1 | 1 | | |
| Rush | 34 | 2 | 3 | | |
| Deane | 27 | 1 | 5 | | 1 |
| Bowyer | 32 | | 4 | | 2 |
| Wetherall | 25 | 4 | | | |
| Tinkler | 1 | 2 | | | |
| Harte | 10 | 4 | 2 | 1 | |
| Hateley | 5 | 1 | | | |
| Gray | 1 | 6 | | | |
| Wallace, Rod | 17 | 5 | 2 | 3 | 2 |
| Blunt | | 1 | | | |
| Jackson | 11 | 6 | | | |
| Boyle | | 1 | | | |
| Dorigo | 15 | 3 | | | |
| Beesley | 11 | 1 | | | |
| Shepherd | 1 | | | | |
| Halle | 20 | | | | |
| Kewell | | 1 | | | |
| Yeboah | 6 | 1 | | | |
| Molenaar | 12 | | 1 | | |
| Beeney | 1 | | | | |
| Lilley | 4 | 2 | | | |
| Laurent | 2 | 2 | | | |

| FA CUP | | | | | |
|---|---|---|---|---|---|
| **Date** | **Team** | **Venue** | **Att** | **Score** | **Scorer** |
| **3rd Round** | | | | | |
| 14 Jan | Crystal Palace | A | 29,486 | 2–2 | Deane, og |
| **3rd Round REPLAY** | | | | | |
| 25 Jan | Crystal Palace | H | 21,903 | 1–0 | Wallace |
| **4th Round** | | | | | |
| 4 Feb | Arsenal | A | 38,115 | 1–0 | Wallace |
| **5th Round** | | | | | |
| 15 Feb | Portsmouth | H | 35,604 | 2–3 | Bowyer 2 |

| COCA-COLA CUP | | | | | |
|---|---|---|---|---|---|
| **Date** | **Team** | **Venue** | **Att** | **Score** | **Scorer** |
| **2nd Round** | | | | | |
| 18 Sept | Darlington | H | 15,230 | 2–2 | Wallace 2 |
| **2nd Round REPLAY** | | | | | |
| 25 Sept | Darlington | A | 6,298 | 2–0 | Wallce, Harte |
| **3rd Round** | | | | | |
| 23 Oct | Aston Villa | H | 15,083 | 1–2 | Sharpe |

# Miscellaneous Premiership Records

## Team Records

| OVERALL RECORD | | | | | | |
|---|---|---|---|---|---|---|
| P | W | D | L | F | A | Pts |
| 202 | 73 | 64 | 65 | 249 | 234 | 283 |

**Win ratio of** 36.14%
**Defeat ratio of** 32.18%
**Strike-rate ratio of** 1.23 goals per game

| HOME RECORD | | | | | | |
|---|---|---|---|---|---|---|
| P | W | D | L | F | A | Pts |
| 101 | 53 | 29 | 19 | 53 | 29 | 188 |

**Win ratio of** 52.5%
**Defeat ratio of** 18.8%

| AWAY RECORD | | | | | | |
|---|---|---|---|---|---|---|
| P | W | D | L | F | A | Pts |
| 101 | 20 | 35 | 46 | 101 | 150 | 95 |

**Win ratio of** 19.8%
**Defeat ratio of 45.5**%
**Strike-rate ratio of** 1 goal per game

### HIGHS AND LOWS

**Biggest victories**

5–0 vs. Tottenham Hotspur (H) 1992–93
5–0 vs. Swindon Town (A) 1993–94

**Heaviest defeats**

5–0 vs. Liverpool (A) 1996–97

**Biggest away victory**

5–0 vs. Swindon Town (A) 1993–94

**Heaviest home defeat**

4–0 vs. Norwich City (H) 1992–93
4–0 vs. Manchester United (H) 1995–96

**Most points**

73 in season 1994–95 (position 5th)

**Fewest points**

43 in season 1995–96 (position 13th)

**Most goals for**

65 in season 1993–94

**Fewest goals for**

40 in season 1995–96

**Most goals against**

62 in season 1992–93

**Fewest goals against**

38 in season 1996–97

**Most victories**

20 in season 1994–95

**Fewest victories**

11 in season 1996–97

**Fewest defeats**

8 in season 1993–94

**Most defeats**

19 in season 1995–96

**Most draws**

16 in season 1993–94

### SEQUENCES AND TOTALS

**Most home wins in a season**

13 games in seasons 1993–94 and 1994–95

**Most home defeats in a season**

8 games in season 1995–96

**Most away wins in a season**

7 games in season 1994–95

**Most away defeats in a season**

14 games in season 1992–93

**Longest unbeaten run**

14 games from 30 August 1993 to 8 December 1993

**Worst run of results**

Six consecutive defeats between 6 April 1996 and 2 May 1996

**Most victories in a row**

5 games in season 1992–93

**Most home victories in a row**

5 games in season 1994–95

**Most away victories in a row**

2 games in season 1993–94 and 1994–95

**Most defeats in a row**

6 games in season 1995–96

### ATTENDANCES

**Highest home attendance**

41,127 vs. Manchester United in season 1993–94

**Highest away attendance**

55,256 vs. Manchester United in season 1996–97

## Individual Records

### GOALSCORING

**Best scoring in a season**

17 goals by Rod Wallace in season 1993–94

**Highest scorer**

Brian Deane 32 goals in 131 (7) appearances

Rod Wallace 32 goals in 124 (22) appearances

**Top scorers per season**

13 goals by Lee Chapman in season 1992–93

17 goals by Rod Wallace in season 1993–94

12 goals by Tony Yeboah in season 1994–95

12 goals by Tony Yeboah in season 1995–96

5 goals by Brian Deane in season 1996–97

**Top five aggregate goalscorers**

Brian Deane 32 goals in 131 (7) appearances

Rod Wallace 32 goals in 124 (22) appearances

Tony Yeboah 24 goals in 44 (3) games

Gary McAllister 24 goals in 151 appearances

Gary Speed 22 goals in 142 (1) appearances

**Most hat-tricks**

Tony Yeboah 2: vs. Ipswich Town (H) 5 April 1995 (won 4–0)

vs. Wimbledon (A) 23 September 1995 (won 4–2)

### APPEARANCES

**Longest run of appearances**

99 by Gary Kelly between 14 August 1993 and 2 December 1995

**Top five aggregate appearances**

1 Gary Kelly 152 (2) appearances

2 Gary McAllister 151 appearances

3 David Wetherall 141 (5) appearances

4 Rod Wallace 124 (22) appearances

5 Gary Speed 142 (1) appearances

# Index

*Italic* page numbers refer to illustrations